DICKENS'S KENT

Dickens's Kent

Peter Clark

First published in Great Britain in 2024 by
The Armchair Traveller
4 Cinnamon Row
London SW11 3TW

Originally published in 2013 as part of *Dickens: London into Kent*

A CIP catalogue record for this book is available from the British Library

Print ISBN: 978-1-914982-11-8
ebook ISBN: 978-1-914982-14-9

Typeset in Garamond by MacGuru Ltd

Cartography produced by ML Design

Maps contain Ordnance Survey data © Crown copyright and database right 2011

Printed in the United Kingdom by Clays Ltd (Elcograf S.p.A.)

The author and the publisher wish to thank the following sources for kind
permission to reproduce the illustrative material:
Graham Salter/Lebrecht Music & Arts, p. 34, p. 76;
Lebrecht Authors, p. 105;
Mary Evans Picture Library, p. 115;
Illustrated London News, p. 125.

Contents

Introduction

I have many happy recollections connected with Kent and am scarcely less interested in it than if I had been a Kentish man bred and born, and had resided in the county all my life.

Charles Dickens, 1840

OUTSIDE LONDON, there is no part of Britain that has such intimate and sustained associations with Charles Dickens as Kent. Dickens's boyhood was restless and nomadic. He accompanied his parents from house to house. His adulthood was not very different – three places in London were his main homes – but Kent was always there as an escape from his life in the capital. In the year after his honeymoon he stayed for several weeks in Broadstairs, the first of many summer and autumn residences in that town. Kent provided the background for some of his first ventures into fiction, in tales that became part of *Sketches by Boz*. Kent was also the inspiration for parts of his first novel *The Pickwick Papers*, written when he was in his early twenties. Some of this novel was written on his honeymoon at Chalk, between Gravesend and Rochester, when he revisited the places that appear so fresh in this early work. Kent provided the foreground of his last, uncompleted, novel, *The Mystery of Edwin Drood*. Indeed, on his last day of consciousness he wrote a beautiful word-picture of the city of Rochester.

His earliest clear memories were of a childhood in and around Chatham, where his father worked in the Navy Pay Office. They were made rosy in retrospect by grim years afterwards, when his father was imprisoned for debt and he worked in the blacking factory, undergoing humiliation, poverty and privation. Chatham fed his emotions and his imagination for the rest of his life. The river, the boats, the navy personnel, the garrison town as well as the buildings, old and new, gave him material that can be detected in most of his fiction. He always had sympathy for men in the services. They may be eccentric, even dotty, but there are no naval or military villains. The personal and geographical landscape of the Medway Towns and their surrounding countryside appear in his first stories, in his own favourite novel, *David Copperfield*, and in his mixture of fiction and journalism, brought together in *The Uncommercial Traveller* and *Reprinted Pieces* as well as in the obvious Kent novels – *Great Expectations* and *The Mystery of Edwin Drood*. Thanet appears in some of his very earliest fiction but did not become the locus of any of his novels. It is as if his Kentish inspiration was based only on places that he had experienced in his childhood.

London and Kent were the two geographical poles of Dickens's exuberant creativity. In *Great Expectations* they are contrasted in the life of Pip; his expectations obliged him to move to London, which is presented as a city of dubious values, hypocrisy and pretence. You had to scheme and negotiate to survive. But Kent represented innocence: the innocence of Pip's childhood, the innocence of Joe Gargery and of Joe's second wife, Biddy. There is much of Dickens in Pip, who, perhaps like his creator, is morally ambiguous. He is vain, seduced by the glamour of becoming a 'gentleman'. His social position turns out to have been based on the wealth of the convict Abel Magwitch, to whom he had, under duress, given comfort as a child. In the last part of the novel, with Magwitch's arrest, the wealth is forfeited to the state. Pip is penniless. The response is hard work, hard work, hard work. Meanwhile the object of his passion, Estella, is (in Dickens's final version) as unobtainable as ever. Life in the Kent village, however, escapes the seductive vanities and corruption of the city. Dickens's last completed novel, *Our Mutual Friend*, implies the same message. In some ways it is his most ambitious novel. London is meretricious and materialistic at every level. In contrast, in *The Mystery of Edwin Drood*, the picture of Rochester is positive. There are absurd people like the mayor, Mr Sapsea, and possible rogues, like John Jasper, but Rochester is best represented by the modest and kindly innocence of the Crisparkles and the Topes.

During Dickens's lifetime there were few changes in the east of the county, but there was a marked transformation in the west, with the development of suburbs and the revolutionary impact of the railways. Instead of being five hours from London, the Medway towns were only one hour away. 'Villadom', as H. G. Wells called it, was spreading into rural Kent. Regardless, the Kent of Dickens's imagination is more static than Dickens's London, and represented for him the ideal of the English countryside. He had a townsman's view of the county – pretty cottages, wild flowers, rolling fields and a stable, harmonious community. The rich were kind to the poor, who knew their place and accepted it. He overlooked some of the darker aspects of contemporary rural poverty and distress, from which Kent was not immune. The Captain Swing riots, with rick-burning and other rural outrages, were taking place in the 1830s. Kent even had the extraordinary event of the Battle of Bossenden Wood in 1838, when disaffected farm labourers were swept up by a messianic charlatan demanding a redistribution of property. But none of this features in Dickens's work. The novels relating most to the county – *Great Expectations* and *The Mystery of Edwin Drood* – reproduce the Kent of Dickens's childhood, and so do the novels that have important Kent chapters – *The Pickwick Papers* and *David Copperfield*.

In *The Pickwick Papers*, we have the story of 'The Old Man's Tale about the Queer Client'. In it, a family is incarcerated – as Dickens's father had been – in Marshalsea prison for debt. A child dies and then the wife. On her deathbed, she begs her husband, 'if ever you leave this dreadful place, and should grow rich, you will have us removed to some quiet country churchyard, a long, long way off – very far from here, where we can rest in peace.' In due course the widower thrives and fulfils the vow he pledged. And 'Beneath a plain grave-stone, in one of the most peaceful and secluded churchyards in Kent, where wild flowers mingle with the grass, and the soft landscape around, forms the fairest spot in the garden of England, lie the bones of the young mother and her gentle child.' In actual fact Kent is physically not 'a long, long way off' from Marshalsea, but for Dickens's purpose it is the emotional and psychological distance that matters.

As he came to maturity, prosperity and celebrity, he expressed more mixed feelings, and even some detachment about London. Although he lived in three houses there for substantial periods, each more spacious than the last, he was never attached to them as he became attached to Gad's Hill Place, near Rochester in Kent: a building he had known, and perhaps coveted, from his childhood. Dickens purchased Gad's Hill Place, which for the rest of his life would be his home, in 1855, where he loved playing the part of benevolent squire and affable host.

But that image was brittle. His personal life was in turmoil. He had left his wife, Catherine, and become besotted with Ellen (Nelly) Ternan, twenty-seven years his junior. He found homes for Nelly first in Slough and later in Peckham (with good train connections to Kent). This affair was known to close family and intimate friends, but was concealed – as was Nelly – from the general public. Around this time, another Kentish site that had a lasting impact on the remainder of Dickens's life was Staplehurst, where he and Nelly were involved in a railway accident. Dickens became a nervous railway passenger ever after. Dickens did all he could to control the narrative of his own private life, destroying personal correspondence and dominating his children. He had to maintain the public image of himself as a moral paragon, the personification of the happy family man. The older children married as soon as they could, escaping from the control-freakery of their father. Sons were educated in France and then dispatched to distant parts of the Empire. Only the eldest daughter, Mary (Mamie) was unquestioningly loyal and devoted to her father.

Dickens died in Kent, at his home at Gad's Hill. In the

generation after his death, several writers traced the physical sites of the buildings and places that appear in his novels. Some of their books had 'tramp' or 'ramble' in their title, and referred to visits to places as 'pilgrimages'. Sometimes Dickens used the names of real places and sites, and it is easy to locate them with precision, such as Cobham or Rochester's cathedral and High Street. But he also slightly disguised the names of other places, or gave them names that are difficult to decode – such as Cloisterham for Rochester in *The Mystery of Edwin Drood*, or Great Winglebury or Dullborough, which are from internal evidence clearly the Medway Towns. At other times he avoided giving place names at all – in *Great Expectations* he was often vague, referring to 'the market town' or 'our village'. It is, however, clear that Rochester and the marshlands were in his mind. And at other times he described one building and switched it to another location; Eastgate House in Rochester becomes Westgate School in Bury St Edmunds in *The Pickwick Papers*. Betsey Trotwood's cottage is based on a house in Broadstairs but is transported to the Dover cliffs. He selects elements from three villages – each described in detail – for the village of Pip's childhood. Dickens was, after all, a creator of fiction. His novels are so persuasive that they read like journalistic reportage but he was under no obligation to be consistent or authentic.

Before the First World War there were several books on Dickens's Kent. I have benefitted from the work of these pioneers. Robert Langton revised details about Dickens's childhood in the Medway towns that had appeared in the first major biography of Charles Dickens by his oldest friend, John Forster. One of the most useful and charming of the early books is *A Week's Tramp in Dickens-land* by the municipal treasurer of the city of Birmingham, William R. Hughes, who, in 1887, travelled with Frederic Kitton, a great Dickens scholar who wrote a good early biography. They travelled around the Medway Towns, tracing people who had known Dickens as a child and as the squire of Gad's Hill. They packed a vast amount of fascinating information into their week. A generation later, one of the greatest Dickens scholars was Walter Dexter. Among his prolific output was a very good book on Dickens and Kent. Laurence Gadd wrote on the *Great Expectations* country. He had clearly walked over much of the lands of the marshes and of the Medway towns. Thanet has received less detailed attention, although Dickens wrote extensively about Broadstairs in his letters to family and friends, and in some journalism.

This book begins by linking Dickens' writings on London and those on Kent. I write about a walk Dickens made in October 1857 as his marriage was collapsing. The years before then were years of triumph, the years after were years of shade. He was walking out of London, where he had had his main residence, to Gad's Hill Place, the house that he had just bought and was to be his home for the rest of his life. It was in some ways as if he was trying to turn his back on the corruption of London and to recapture the tranquillity of his Kentish childhood. The book continues into the areas in Kent most closely associated with the life and work of Dickens – the Medway Towns and their surroundings, Thanet and East Kent and finally Staplehurst, the scene of the railway accident that nearly killed him.

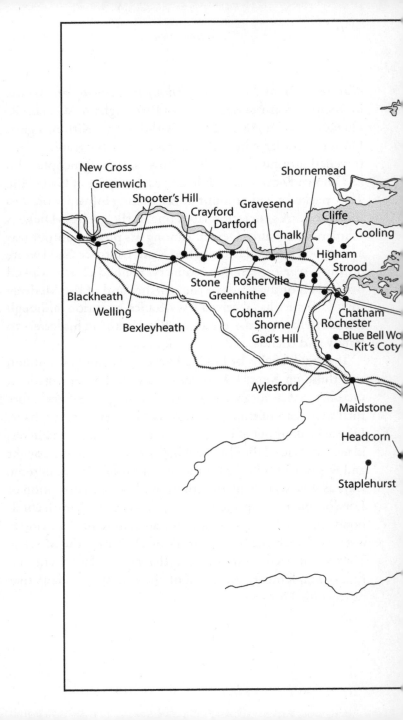

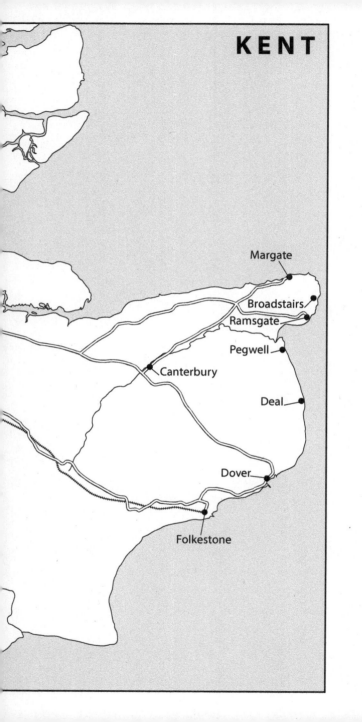

KENT

Margate

Broadstairs

Ramsgate

Pegwell

Canterbury

Deal

Dover

Folkestone

London into Kent

My last special feat was turning out of bed at two, after a hard day, pedestrian and otherwise, and walking thirty miles into the country to breakfast. The road was so lonely in the night that I fell asleep to the monotonous sound of my own feet, doing their regular four miles an hour. Mile after mile I walked, without the slightest sense of exertion, dozing heavily and dreaming constantly. It was only when I made a stumble like a drunken man, or struck out into the road to avoid a horseman close upon me on the path – who had no existence – that I came to myself and looked about.

THUS WROTE CHARLES DICKENS, in an 1860 article 'Shy Neighbourhoods', which appeared in the magazine he edited (or, as he said, 'conducted'), *All the Year Round*. The thirty-mile walk referred to a trek he made from central London in October 1857 to his recently acquired house at Gad's Hill between Rochester and Gravesend. Dickens was forty-five years old, at the height of his fame. The timing of the walk is significant.

It seems probable that Dickens undertook the walk – the authorities are not unanimous – on the night of either Tuesday 14 or Wednesday 15 October 1857. The moon would have been entering its last quarter, and meteorological records indicate that it was foggy at dawn and overcast later in the day. But then, as Dickens himself has described, London was notorious for its fogs. Dickens always walked briskly, maintaining a steady pace and rarely stopping. We have a description of the way Dickens walked from a resident of Strood who often saw him walking from Gad's Hill into Rochester. He usually wore

low shoes not over-well mended, loose large check-patterned trousers that sometimes got entangled in those shoes when walking, a house coat thrown open, sometimes without waistcoat, a belt instead of braces, a necktie which now and then got round towards his ear, and a large-brimmed felt hat, similar to an American's, set well at the back of his head. In his hand he carried by the middle an umbrella, which he was in the habit of constantly swinging ... he walked in the middle of the road at a rapid pace, upright, but with his eyes cast down as if deep in thought.

His eldest son, Charley, also recalled walking with him:

Many a mile have I walked with him thus – he striding along with his regular four-miles-an-hour swing; his eyes looking straight before him, his lips slightly working, as they generally did when he sat thinking and writing; almost unconscious of companionship, and keeping half a pace or so ahead. When he had worked out what had come into his mind he would drop back again into line – again, I am sure, almost unconsciously – and the conversation would be resumed, as if there had been no appreciable break or interval at all.

There was, however, something special about the night walk of the autumn of 1857. In August that year he had become infatuated with the actress Ellen (Nelly) Ternan. In September he had gone on a walking tour in the north of England with Wilkie Collins, 'the walking tour of two idle apprentices' and just happened to turn up for the races at Doncaster where Nelly was performing in the theatre. A few days before the walk he instructed his wife's confidential maid to convert his dressing room at his house at Tavistock Square into his bedroom and to block the door between that room and his former marital bedroom with bookshelves. This was a most symbolic gesture after years of increasing alienation from his wife, Catherine. There had been flirtations for ten years or more, and in 1855 Maria Beadnell, his first flame, now Mrs Winter, had got in contact with him. Memories of his first love excited him but meeting up with her was a bitter disappointment and Dickens portrayed her with callous savagery as Flora Finching in *Little Dorrit*.

In the late spring of the following year, 1858, Dickens formally, publicly and brutally dumped Catherine.

Edgar Johnson's biography of 1952 summarises Dickens's life with the subtitle, *His Tragedy and Triumph*. Until the late 1850s his adult life had been constant triumph. With the serialisation of *The Pickwick Papers* at the age of twenty-four he became instantly famous, and celebrity followed him for the rest of his life. The twelve years before his death were the years of tragedy. Although Nelly became his lover, Dickens had to keep it secret and was sometimes furtive in his public movements, and with the collapse of his marriage he lost friends. There were several other personal changes. In the years of his triumph his closest friend was John Forster, his biographer. Like Dickens, Forster was a lower-middle-class lad from the provinces – in his case Newcastle-upon-Tyne – who arrived in London and immediately became an important figure in the literary world. He was an excellent man of business, with a legal training, who gained the confidence of writers a generation or so older – such as Charles Lamb and Walter Savage Landor – and looked after their affairs. Both Dickens and Forster walked tall in literary London while still in their mid-twenties. Forster was distressed at the marital breakdown and Dickens did not always follow his advice. Relations cooled in the late 1850s, and Forster was replaced as an intimate by the novelist Wilkie Collins, Dickens's junior by eleven years. Collins was the son and brother of Royal Academicians. He responded to the raffish side of Dickens's character, managing a life with two mistresses simultaneously. Dickens and Collins spent holidays together in Paris, and collaborated on writing. Dickens never cut off relations with Forster, who wrote the affectionate early biography, but was impatient with a prissiness in Forster's character; the character of Podsnap, the self-righteous and insular character in *Our Mutual Friend*, is generally believed to have been based on Forster.

In the years after 1857 Dickens took up, against the advice of John Forster, his new career of paid public readings. Thereafter he was constantly on the move. He found homes for Nelly first in Slough and then in Peckham, adopted false names and really behaved like a character in one of his own novels. It was at this time that he grew the beard. He had grown a beard before for theatrical performances or temporarily on holiday, but after 1857 his beard became a fixed feature. Although beards had become more fashionable after the Crimean War, it was as if Dickens was adopting a disguise from the familiar open and sensual features of his early manhood, so iconically captured in Daniel Maclise's portrait of 1839.

The route of the 1857 walk was symbolic. Dickens had leased Tavistock House, Tavistock Square, since 1851. The building has since been replaced by the current headquarters of the British Medical Association. Tavistock House had been the family home, where his ten children – of whom one died as an infant – lived and where he entertained. It was the domain of his wife, Catherine. In 1855 he bought Gad's Hill Place, the house of his childhood dreams. He spent much of the following year making changes to the house, often staying at the Sir John Falstaff inn opposite. Although Catherine stayed at Gad's Hill once, it was very much Charles's house and was to become his base for the rest of his life. So the walk was a move from one building that represented his life of the previous twenty-one years, to another building that was to represent the following thirteen.

Dickens was not alone among the great Victorians in being a strenuous walker; others also used to eat up the miles. George Borrow could walk up to sixty miles in a day, striding along at six miles an hour. Prime Minister William Gladstone walked dozens of miles across England and Scotland. He would record the distances covered in his journal with obsessive precision – '34¾ miles'. Gladstone also walked around London at night, rescuing prostitutes. An older contemporary, the historian Thomas Macaulay (born in 1800), also used to pace the streets of the capital. Macaulay reckoned that in his youth he had walked along every London street. In the years after 1820

London underwent a rapid expansion and such a claim would no longer have been plausible.

In the previous century, long-distance cross-country walking was regarded as a bit odd, a socially inferior practice. Before the coming of the railways there were four principal methods of long-distance journeying. The socially superior would have their own vehicles of various degrees of expense and elaborateness. Below that, the highest form of public transport was the stagecoach, which had its glory days in the first thirty years of the nineteenth century, between the organisation of roads through the turnpike trusts and the coming of the railways (or 'railroads', as Dickens called them). Dickens recorded and celebrated this final age of the stagecoach in many of his early works such as *The Pickwick Papers* and *Nicholas Nickleby*. Travel was exhausting, uncomfortable, hazardous and time-consuming, but there was a network of support, with the coaching inns, relays of horses and coach craftsmen ready to repair or replace. Below the stagecoaches – socially – were the wagons: slow, friendly and also uncomfortable. And below all of them were the pedestrians. This was particularly the case in England; less so in Wales or Scotland.

One visitor to England at the end of the eighteenth century observed that a 'traveller on foot in this country seems to be considered as a sort of wild man, or an out-of-the-way being, who is stared at, pitied, suspected, and shunned by everybody that meets him.'

The traveller on foot did not eat in the main dining room of a public house but was often directed to eat in the kitchen with the domestic staff. This had clearly changed by the 1830s; it is hard to imagine the young Gladstone being directed to the kitchen. But by then walking long distances had become more socially acceptable for middle class intellectuals. The cause may have been the influence of William Wordsworth, who was poet laureate from 1834 to 1850. He had drawn attention to the beauties of Britain and his rambles, whether past Tintern Abbey or in the Lake District, chimed with a romantically inclined reading public.

For many in London, however, walking was an essential part of daily life. In the years after the Napoleonic wars London expanded and new inner suburbs grew north of what was known as New Road, now the road that passes by the northern railway termini – Marylebone, Baker Street, Euston and Kings Cross/St Pancras. People lived here and walked to offices in the cities of London and Westminster. In an early paper that appeared in *Sketches by Boz*, Dickens noted how

> the early clerk population of Somers and Camden towns, Islington, and Pentonville, are fast pouring into the city; or directing their steps towards Chancery-lane and the Inns of Court. Middle-aged men, whose salaries have by no means increased in the same proportion as their families, plod steadily along, apparently with no object in view but the counting-house; knowing by sight almost every body they meet or overtake, for they have seen them every morning (Sundays excepted) during the past twenty years, but speaking to no one.

In Dickens's novels there are several accounts of long walks; there was nothing exceptional about them. Sam Weller, when he goes to see his father and stepmother in Dorking, walks all the way back to London. Traddles in *David Copperfield* almost incidentally mentions that he walked from London to Devonshire to see his fiancée, the 'dearest girl in the world'. Oliver Twist at the age of eleven walked from Mudfog, seventy miles north of London, to the capital, covering twenty miles in the first day. David Copperfield at about the same age walked from London to Dover, walking twenty-three miles in one day from Blackheath to Chatham. Pip in *Great Expectations*, when he learnt that Estella was to marry Bentley Drummle, walked in despair back to London from – one presumes – Rochester. Later in the book he travelled by stagecoach but alighted at the Half-way House, and 'breakfasted there, and walked the rest of the distance'. Nell and her grandfather in *The Old Curiosity Shop* wander largely on foot from the capital to the West Midlands. Nicholas Nickleby and Smike walk the greater part of the way from London to Portsmouth. On the first day they walked thirty miles from London to Godalming. Given Smike's physical frailty this seems improbable. More improbable is the twenty-five miles alleged to have been walked by Mr Pickwick and his companions, after having enjoyed a lavish and bibulous wedding breakfast at Dingley Dell in December.

Apart from that night in 1857 I do not think Dickens walked thirty miles in one day (or night). Regularly he walked ten or twelve miles in a day; sometimes twenty. A methodical man, his habit was to write every morning for four hours, and then walk for four hours. He had the idea that hours given to intellectual labour should correspond to hours spent in strenuous physical exercise, in his case, walking. But there was, even for Dickens, something exceptional about the night walk into Kent in October 1857. I think it was, in fact, the turning point of his life. In spite of his assertion that he was half-asleep during the walk, I think his mind may well have been actively reassessing his life.

As I read about and reflected on Dickens's walk, I decided that I would like to repeat it, also leaving Tavistock Square at two in the morning. I suggested the idea to my wife, Theresa. She was alarmed and thought that I was crazy to walk in the middle of the night through what she saw as some of the dodgiest parts of London. I did some research. It appears that the London boroughs with the lowest crime rates were Greenwich and Bexley. By contrast, the Cities of London and Westminster and the Royal Borough of Kensington and Chelsea were the most crime-ridden boroughs. Southwark and Lambeth were average. But I also sought advice. I telephoned Southwark Police to discuss the idea of the walk. I explained that it was in the steps of Charles Dickens and they were immediately empathetic and helpful. I should not go alone, they advised. Nor at the weekend. The Elephant and Castle area was notorious for muggings. The riskiest time was when the clubs closed – about 3:00 a.m. along the Old Kent Road. The clubs were usually open at weekends. I found two friends to go with me – Robin and Les – and we agreed to go mid-week. Meanwhile I did a recce of the area during the daytime. I went to Elephant and Castle to check where we could best cross the roads, avoiding the subway, and I dropped in on shops and cafes on the Old Kent Road to ask what it was like there at 3:00 and 4:00 in the morning. There was always a trickle of traffic and people around, I was told. This was reassuring, at least for me, even if Theresa was not totally convinced.

In determining which route to take, I consulted Victorian

maps. I wanted to follow the route Dickens was most likely to have taken. Although Tavistock Square was where he had his family house, he also kept a bachelor pad above the offices of his magazine, *Household Words*, in Wellington Street off the Strand. On Pip's walk in the opposite direction in *Great Expectations*, he crossed over London Bridge, but Blackfriars Bridge or Waterloo Bridge would have made sense if Dickens was setting out either from Wellington Street or Tavistock Square. Dickens was always careful with his money and in 1857 Waterloo Bridge was still levying a toll on pedestrians crossing. Dickens would, I guessed, have opted for the free bridge. We therefore decided to cross the river by Blackfriars Bridge. He probably went by St George's Obelisk, the junction south of the Thames of roads going to London Bridge, Blackfriars and Westminster. The route from there to Gad's Hill is straight-forward – to the Elephant and Castle, the Bricklayers' Arms, along the old Watling Street to Blackheath, Shooter's Hill, Welling, Bexleyheath, Crayford, Dartford and by the Old Dover Road skirting the south of Gravesend.

So one night in November 2011 Robin's wife dropped the three of us off at Tavistock Square at 2:00 in the morning and we set off, walking past Dickens's earlier home in Doughty Street, by Ludgate Circus, and crossing the Thames by Black-friars Bridge. St George's Circus was on the edge of the built-up area in the 1850s. There were a few buildings to the south, including Walcot Square, where Mr Guppy in *Bleak House* lived.

We sped by the Elephant and Castle and along the Old Kent Road, the old Watling Street. There was indeed a constant flow of traffic and few pedestrians in these wee hours. Buses passed by, their passengers mostly asleep. It was as if zombies were being transported across the capital. Shops indicated a culturally diverse population and the Old Kent Road seemed to be full of Pentecostal churches. Signs pointed to Peckham on the right, and we thought of the house Dickens bought for Nelly. It was on a good train line – into central London and also handy for Rochester. In her biography of Ellen Ternan, Claire Tomalin speculates on one story that Dickens's fatal stroke occurred there and not at Gad's Hill, the body being transported by cart to Gad's Hill in the dead of night, if that is not too inappropriate a phrase.

We were getting into our stride. There wasn't much conversation along a road that was unfamiliar to any of us. At New Cross we entered the old county of Kent and started to climb. Suddenly we came to the open level space of Blackheath. We had left the dodgier parts of London and were about to enter gracious inner suburbia. We had met no potential muggers but were accosted, I think, by a lady of the night, although Les firmly (and perhaps gallantly) denied she was. We were ready for a break – we had walked seven or eight miles and it was nearly 4:00 a.m. To our surprise and delight we found the Blackheath Tea Hut, an all-night café. We joined some jolly policemen celebrating the birthday of one of their colleagues with tea and baps.

Opposite the Tea Hut was the walk down to Greenwich, 'the long vista of gnarled old trees in Greenwich Park', as Dickens called it in his Christmas story 'The Seven Poor Travellers'.

David Copperfield also paused at Blackheath on his walk to Dover. The school he had attended, Salem House, where he had met Steerforth and Traddles, was at Blackheath – the exact location is uncertain – and on his walk David spent a night sleeping rough near the familiar buildings of the school. Blackheath overlooks Greenwich Park where Dickens, in 1835 at the age of twenty-three, wrote a delightful early piece, later appearing in *Sketches by Boz*, on the unrestrained enjoyments of Greenwich Fair.

It was still dark when we resumed after our break. Did Dickens have a break? There may have been hostelries where he might have had a glass of something to spur him on.

Blackheath in the eighteenth century – along with Shooter's Hill and Bexleyheath – had a reputation for highway robbery. The road was famed for 'the unmerciful plundering of travellers'. Passengers on the night coach to Dover in the second chapter of *A Tale of Two Cities* were nervous of highwaymen when, on a late November night, the coach carrying Jarvis Lorry was 'lumbering up' and was stopped by a horseman with an urgent message. Fear gripped crew and passengers, 'the guard suspected the passengers, the passengers suspected one another and the guards, they all suspected everybody else, and the coachman was sure of nothing but the horses.' The gradient was steep and passengers had dismounted from the coach, 'not because they had the least relish for walking exercise, under the circumstances, but because the hill, and the harness, and the mud, and the mail, were all so heavy, that the horses had three times already come to a stop, besides once drawing the coach across the road, with the mutinous intent of taking it back to Blackheath.' At the summit of Shooter's Hill, just beyond the Victorian Gothic water tower, was a pub, The Bull, rebuilt in the 1880s. Its predecessor was a coaching inn, built in 1749, which would have been familiar to Charles Dickens.

Tony Weller, Sam's father in *The Pickwick Papers*, retired to near Shooter's Hill.

The road was as straight as an arrow's flight as we paced along the route of the Roman road through Welling, Bexleyheath and Crayford. I observed a strange phenomenon in these dormitory towns: an extraordinary number of nail bars. We passed three in Welling and five in Bexleyheath but only one in Crayford. Dawn was beginning to break and we were heartened by a phone call from my wife, Theresa, at 6:30 a.m. She was relieved to learn that we had not been beset by footpads. We were cheered on for the rest of the walk.

We wondered how the dawn would have been for Dickens. He does describe a similar dawn as Oliver Twist walked into London from Bethnal Green with Bill Sikes, en route to the burglary in Chertsey:

> The day had fairly begun to break. Many of the lamps were already extinguished, a few country wagons were slowly toiling on towards London, and now and then a stage-coach, covered with mud, rattled briskly by ... The public-houses, with gas-lights burning inside, were already open. By degrees other shops began to be unclosed, and a few scattered people were met with. Then came struggling groups of labourers going to their work; then men and women with fish-baskets on their heads, donkey-carts laden with vegetables, chaise-carts filled with live-stock or whole carcasses of meat, milkwomen with pails, and an unbroken concourse of people trudging out with supplies to the eastern suburbs of the town.

There are several points to make here. *Oliver Twist* was written twenty years before the 1857 walk and Bethnal Green is described as if it is in the country, whereas maps of the time show a continuous built-up area. The Oliver walk was, I think, in late spring, rather than October. And between the 1830s and the 1850s the railways had arrived. (Indeed, during our walk, we were comforted by the fact that if it was too much for us, we were never more than two miles from a railway station and that from 6:00 in the morning there would be commuter trains that could take us into central London.) Dickens might well have encountered carts bringing fresh produce into London or to the market centres in the south-east of the metropolis. Although the railways totally changed the transportation of fresh milk, fruit and vegetables, it was not always on an industrial scale; smaller cultivators continued to use horse-drawn carts. So the account in *Oliver Twist* might broadly have described Dickens's walk in 1857.

Dickens was familiar with this route, which gets several mentions in his novels. Mr Dorrit, after his release from Marshalsea, set out on this road. In *The Pickwick Papers*, Dickens tells a story – or Tony Weller does – about two coachmen who saluted each other with a 'jerking round of the right wrist and a rising of the little finger into the air at the same time. They were twins, between whom an unaffected and devoted attachment existed. They passed each other on the Dover Road, every day, for twenty-four years, never exchanging any other greeting than this; and yet, when one died, the other pined away, and soon afterwards followed him.'

I had arranged to call at the house of my friend Hassan at Crayford at about 7:00 a.m. We were half an hour late, but what a welcome break it was. We sat in comfortable chairs, sipping Somali coffee – Hassan's wife is Somali. We asked Hassan about the nail bars. There was a simple explanation, he told us. Vietnamese refugees had been settled at Thamesmead, east of Greenwich. They had cornered such a market as there was in nail bars in north-west Kent.

We had to tear ourselves away from the armchairs and move on; Crayford and then on to Dartford. Though traffic is diverted away from the centre, Dartford is the first place east of London which seemed to have its own character, rather than being just a dormitory suburb of the capital. Like Rochester, it has a Royal Victoria and Bull Hotel, where, a plaque declares, the steam locomotive pioneer, Robert Trevithick, lived and died. We were entering Dickens country, for Dartford has a Copperfield Market and a Pickwick Pawnbrokers.

The north Kentish coast has reminders of a medieval royal importance. Greenwich and Eltham had palaces, and travellers, royal and common, used to travel to continental Europe by the River Thames in boats that hugged the shore, landing for supplies or ceremonies. At Dartford, King Henry V stopped to give thanks in the church for his victory at Agincourt.

Today the coastline has been disfigured by the chalk quarries and half-abandoned industrial sites. The industries were mostly for the production of cement and paper. Cement was developed here from the late eighteenth century, the industry being fed from the local chalk. Unruly capitalism had its wicked way with the virgin landscape and moved on. Today huge acres consist of a jungle of squalor, though in some of the old villages near the shore are blocks of flats that would wish to be seen as luxury accommodation.

Walking on a high bridge over the M25 seemed to be symbolic, though this stretch of the orbital road is not actually a motorway. We were breaking through the chain that fettered the capital. On the eastern side we could look across meadows where horses were grazing, arched by the Dartford Bridge, with an oil refinery on the northern bank of the River Thames, busy with freight-bearing craft – a mix of rural England, industry and modern transport networks.

Beyond the bridge is another area of sad development that conceals the treasure of the church at Stone and the old coastal village of Greenhithe. The landscape is post-industrial, the last factory having been closed down in 2010. Greenhithe has two parts – a residential area and a marina dating from not earlier than the 1980s. It was once a pretty little fishing village, with a pier in the eighteenth century. In Dickens's time it attracted visitors who arrived by paddle-steamer to enjoy what one tourist book described as Greenhithe's 'rural and sylvan scenes'. It provided moorage for a yacht owned by Mr Tartar in *The Mystery of Edwin Drood*. Beyond the pier an older village spreads round the Sir John Franklin public house. Franklin was a Lincolnshire man, a naval officer, and an explorer who died with his men in seeking the North West Passage in 1845. The whole expedition perished. Local First Nations people maintained that the expedition resorted to cannibalism before perishing. These reports led, understandably, to huge controversy in Britain. Franklin's widow repudiated the notion; her husband was 'clean, Christian and genteel', she declared. Dickens entered the controversy, repudiating the Inuit evidence. 'We believe every savage in his heart to be covetous, treacherous, and cruel: and we have yet to learn what knowledge the white man – lost, houseless, ship-less, apparently forgotten by his race, plainly famine-stricken, weak, frozen and dying – has of the gentleness of Exquimaux.' The story of Franklin inspired Wilkie Collins and Dickens to write a play, *The Frozen Deep*. This was put on in early 1857 with an amateur cast, including Dickens's daughters. It had huge social success. When Dickens's friend, Douglas Jerrold, died later that year, Dickens came up with the idea of perform-ing the play to raise funds for Jerrold's widow and family. He, of course, played the central character. One performance was attended by Queen Victoria. Collins and Dickens decided to put on money-spinning performances at the Free Trade Hall, Manchester, in August. A larger venue called for the employ-ment of professional actresses rather than Dickens's own daughters. One of the actresses recruited was Ellen Ternan. This was the genesis of Dickens's infatuation and the begin-ning of the upheavals in his life.

Seven or eight miles after leaving Crayford, we stopped for a third breakfast at a greasy spoon on the western outskirts of Gravesend, before the final haul. The Old Dover Road took us along the southern fringes of Gravesend. Between this road and the Thames was Rosherville Gardens, pleasure gardens in Dickens's time. 'Ah Rosherville! That fated Rosherville, when shall we see it?' Dickens wrote in a letter in 1847, when the gardens had been open for ten years, replacing disused chalk quarries. Paddle-steamers brought day trippers from London to a special pier. The gardens, with an archery ground, a maze, a conservatory, and a 'bijou' theatre were there for the delight of trippers. There was even a zoo with elephants and a bear pit. The gardens were founded in 1837 and lingered on until the 1930s, but the heyday was late Victorian times. Rosher-ville later became another insensitive industrial site and there is little to see of its earlier glories. All that is left of the pier are stumps in the ground with a commemorative plaque. One of the industries that took over the area was Henley's Electric Cable Works. Their art deco headquarters survives but is boarded up, ripe for demolition.

Gravesend featured in Dickens's life and work, but not to the extent that Rochester did. The docks at Tilbury were built in the 1880s, but early in the century Gravesend had been a resort and a major port. It features occasionally in Dickens's work. Mr Pickwick and his colleagues walked to Gravesend from Cobham. It was one of the places the law clerks in *Bleak House* would visit as day trippers from London. The tripper traffic expanded enormously during Dickens's youth. In 1821 27,000 people disembarked each year at Gravesend. Ten years later the figure was almost a quarter of a million. The elegant Town Pier built in 1834 to deal with this traffic still survives. It was also a port for boats from other parts of the east coast of Britain. When Peggotty and Ham visited David Copperfield at Blackheath they came to Gravesend from Yarmouth 'in one of our Yarmouth lugs'. It was also a port of embarkation for places abroad. Gravesend was where Walter Gay and his bride, Florence, in *Dombey and Son*, set off on their honeymoon. When Mr Peggotty emigrated to Australia with Mr Micawber, it was from Gravesend that they set off. Australia was, in Dickens's imagination, a continent of adventure and opportunity. Both Micawber and Magwitch transformed their lives and prospered in Australia. Micawber went as a voluntary emigrant, Magwitch as a transported criminal. Dickens, who despaired of what he saw as the fecklessness of his sons – inherited, he claimed, of course from their mother – sent two of his sons to Australia to farm and trade. In the 1860s he entertained the idea of visiting Australia himself to give readings and make money.

Gravesend was more than a people's port of embarkation or disembarkation. Here in 1863 Princess Alexandra of Denmark came onto English soil to marry Queen Victoria's eldest son, the Prince of Wales. The second pier, the Terrace Pier, became the Royal Terrace Pier thereafter.

Dickens knew Gravesend as a boy, living at Chatham, and as a newly-wed, honeymooning at Chalk nearby. On the shore near the canal built to connect the Thames and the Medway he would have seen a house that had an upturned boat serving as a roof. This clearly stuck in his mind when in 1849 he wrote in *David Copperfield* of the Peggotty household in Great Yarmouth. The house lasted until 1924. When his house at Gad's Hill was undergoing the changes he insisted on, Dickens stayed at Waits Hotel in the town. This later became the Commercial Hotel but no trace survives. The town also has memories of that other great Victorian, General Charles George Gordon, who, as a Royal Engineer in the late 1860s, worked on the Thames fortresses that defended the approach to the capital. He did charitable work, teaching at 'ragged schools' and founding a boys' club. Did Dickens and Gordon ever meet?

Dickens was commemorated in the naming of two of the passenger ferry boats that plied between Gravesend and Tilbury at the turn of the twenty-first century: a locally built catamaran was named *Great Expectations* and a trimaran *Martin Chuzzlewit*.

We walked along the southern outskirts of Gravesend, joining the main road to Rochester, built in the twentieth century. We could have gone straight ahead – as Dickens certainly would have done – through the village of Chalk, past the weather-boarded cottage where, in happier marital days, he had spent his honeymoon with Catherine. A plaque on the cottage commemorates the honeymoon. Chalk also claims the origin of the forge in *Great Expectations*; this stands, fittingly, in Forge Lane. It adjoined the house, which 'was a wooden house, as many of the dwellings in our country were'. Some early numbers of *The Pickwick Papers* were written in Chalk; hence the freshness of the Rochester chapters.

We were tired and, rather than diverting through Chalk, chose the boring slog up to Gad's Hill, reaching the Sir John Falstaff pub, opposite Dickens's home, Gad's Hill Place.

The walk had taken us twelve hours. When Pip in *Great Expectations* travelled by coach to London, the journey took five hours. Dickens in 1857 had covered the distance on foot in seven. But then Dickens in 1857 was 45 and the combined age of the three of us was 194.

Gad's Hill

It was midway between Gravesend and Rochester, and the widening river was bearing the ships, white-sailed or black-smoked, out to sea, when I noticed by the wayside a very queer small boy.

'Holloa!' said I, to the very queer small boy, 'where do you live?'

'At Chatham,' says he.

'What do you do there?' says I.

'I go to school,' says he.

I took him up in a moment, and we went on. Presently the very queer small boy says, 'This is Gads-hill we are coming to, where Falstaff went out to rob those travellers, and ran away.'

'You know something about Falstaff, eh?' said I.

'All about him,' said the very queer small boy. 'I am old (I am nine), and I read all sorts of books. But let us stop at the top of the hill, and look at the house there, if you please!'

'You admire the house?' said I.

'Bless you, sir,' says the very queer small boy, 'when I was not more than half as old as nine, it used to be a treat for me to be brought to look at it. And now, I am nine, I come by myself to look at it. And ever since I can recollect, my father, seeing me so fond of it, has often said to me, "If you were to be very persevering and were to work hard, you might some day come to live in it.'"

Dickens wrote this whimsical account, imagining his own self as a boy, wistfully coveting 'the house' in 1860 for *All the Year Round*; it was later reprinted in *The Uncommercial Traveller.* He had bought the house – Gad's Hill Place – in 1855. At first he bought it as much as an investment as a possible residence, and indeed in the first year of ownership did let it out. But after the breakdown of his marriage it became his main home for the rest of his life.

Dickens was thrilled by the literary associations with Gad's Hill. It was on one of the pilgrim routes between London and Canterbury and he savoured the idea that Chaucer's pilgrims passed by the house. Canterbury pilgrims were the potential victims of Falstaff's robbery in Shakespeare's King Henry IV Part One: 'Lads, tomorrow morning, by four o'clock, early at Gadshill! There are pilgrims going to Canterbury with rich offerings, and traders riding to London with fat purses.'

The road between Rochester and Gravesend was probably the busiest in Kent in the eighteenth and into the nineteenth century. Gravesend was a major domestic port, conveying merchandise to and from Kent. Travellers for Rochester, Canterbury, Dover and the continent often went by boat to Gravesend and onward by road. It was the second road in the county to be managed by a turnpike trust and so had milestones from the eighteenth century. As Mr F's aunt in *Little Dorrit* said, 'There's milestones on the Dover Road'.

Dickens felt a sense of history about the Dover Road, over which 'the old Romans used to march, over where the old Canterbury pilgrims used to go, over the road where the travelling trains of the old imperious priests and princes used to jingle on horseback between the Continent and this Island through the mud and water, over the road where Shakespeare hummed to himself, "Blow, blow, thou winter wind."'

Dickens was an acute observer of the wayfarers on this road. He noted the tramps – scoundrels, men and women living off their wits, the shabby genteel, reduced gentlefolk. There were also itinerant craftsmen, tinkers, chair-menders, umbrella-menders, clock-menders, knife-grinders. And then the seasonal migrations: haymakers in the early summer and hop-pickers from elsewhere. 'Many of these hoppers are Irish, but many come from London.' Kent provided a working holiday for people from East London until the 1960s.

The house, Gad's Hill Place – in his correspondence he often referred to it as 'Gad's' – was initially known as Gad's Hill House, and was built in about 1780 by Thomas Stephens, successively ostler, brewer and mayor of Rochester. After he died, the house had several owners and occupiers until 1827 when the Reverend James Lynn acquired the freehold and for a while lived in it. His daughter, Eliza, was a free thinker, wrote a novel – *Joshua Davidson* – based on the Gospel story and wrote for several journals, including Dickens's own *Household Words*. After her father died, she inherited the house. By one of those coincidences that would be stretching credibility if they occurred in a Dickens novel, Miss Lynn met W. H. Wills, the assistant editor of *Household Words*, at a dinner party at the beginning of February 1855. She told him she had just

Gad's Hill Place

inherited Gad's Hill Place and wanted to sell it. Wills immediately told Dickens, who he knew was interested in the property. Dickens entered negotiations to purchase the place. The
house had already appeared – it is reasonable to surmise – in
his own fiction. In *A Christmas Carol*, written in 1843, Scrooge
and the Spirit of Christmas Past visited the scenes of Scrooge's
childhood and 'approached a mansion of dull red brick, with
a little weathercock – surmounted cupola on the roof, and a
bell hanging in it.'

Dickens's younger sister, Letitia, had married an architect and surveyor, Henry Austin. He came to Gad's Hill and
checked the foundations, roof and drainage. All seemed to be

in order but negotiations were prolonged. Miss Lynn wanted £2,000, Henry Austin suggested £1,700. They agreed on £1,700–1,790 for the house and £90 for an area of derelict land on the other side of the road.

In March 1856 Dickens became the owner of 'my little Kentish free-hold'. The house was already occupied by a tenant, the rector of Higham, the Reverend Joseph Hindle. His lease did not expire for another year. Dickens agreed for him to see out the lease. Dickens had big plans for decorating and furnishing the house. 'It is so old-fashioned, plain, and comfortable', he wrote to his friend, Baroness Burdett-Coutts:

On the summit of Gad's Hill, with a noble prospect at the side and behind, looking down into the Valley of the Medway. Lord Darnley's Park at Cobham (a beautiful place with a noble walk through the wood) is close by it; and Rochester is within a mile or two. It is only an hour and a quarter from London by the Railway. [150 years later the train from Higham to Charing Cross takes an hour and four minutes.] To crown all, the sign of the Sir John Falstaff is over the way, and I used to look at it as a wonderful Mansion (which God knows it is not), when I was a very odd child with the first faint shadows of all my books in my head – I suppose.

Initially he moved in only for the summer, retaining Tavistock House until 1860. After that Gad's Hill became his principal residence.

Dickens had the plot of land across the road planted as a shrubbery and it became known as the Wilderness. In Dickens's time it was dominated by two huge cedar trees, planted about the time the house was built. In 1907 storms severely damaged them and they were felled. Fresh cedars have been planted to replace them. One of Dickens's favourite dogs, the St Bernard Linda, is buried in the Wilderness. And it was in the Wilderness that Dickens placed the chalet that had been a gift from the French actor, Charles Fechter, in 1864. It arrived at Gad's Hill in fifty-eight packing cases containing ninety-four pieces and, like a complex piece of IKEA furniture, had to be assembled. 'My room is up among the branches of the trees,' he wrote to an American friend, 'and the birds and the butterflies fly in and out, and the green branches shoot in at the open windows, and the lights and shadows of the clouds come and go with the rest of the company.'

Dickens had a tunnel constructed under the road connecting the front garden of the house to the Wilderness in 1865. It is no longer used but the entrance and steps can be seen from the public footpath. During the Second World War it became a comfortable First Aid Post.

As soon as he moved into the house Dickens organised a house-warming party, arranging for guests to come from London by train, to Higham Station, a mile and a quarter away. (The station is undistinguished but the train, heading for Rochester, plunges into a long two-mile tunnel. Whereby hangs a tale. This tunnel was originally built between 1819 and 1824 for a canal. The designer was William Tierney Clark, the architect-engineer who also designed the suspension bridge over the Thames at Marlow, which was a prototype of his internationally best-known work, the 1839 iron suspension bridge over the Danube at Budapest. The South Eastern

Railway Company bought up the canal in 1844, filled it in and laid the railway line in its place. Traces of the canal that linked Gravesend with the Medway at Strood can still be seen in Lower Higham village.)

Dickens had brought his books and other personal effects from Tavistock House. Among these were the dummy book-cases, concealing the entrance to his study. The book titles on the dummy bookcase included *The History of a Short Chancery Suit* in twenty-seven volumes and *Cat's Lives* in nine volumes. Another set of dummy books was the *Catalogue of Statues of the Duke of Wellington* in ten volumes. This reveals one of Dickens's prejudices – not against the Duke of Wellington, but against such memorials to the living or the dead. In his will he conjured 'my friends on no account to make me the subject of any monument, memorial, or testimonial whatever. I rest my claims to the remembrance of my country upon my published works, and to the remembrance of my friends upon their experience of me in addition thereto'. In accordance with his wishes no statue was erected to Dickens after his death. That is, until the summer of 2013 when, in defiance of his wishes, a statue was erected and unveiled at the city of his birthplace, Portsmouth. This is the first in Britain – though there are statues of Dickens in Sydney, Australia, and Philadelphia, in the United States.

When he was at Gad's Hill he wrote in the library, the room that is on the ground floor to the right of the porch as you face the building. After 1865 when he had the chalet he worked there during the summer mornings. He was methodical, and wrote with a quill on blue paper. He was short-sighted and wore gold-rimmed spectacles when at work; curiously, none of the pictures of him show him wearing glasses – unlike Thackeray, for example.

He brought other things from Tavistock House. He was almost fetishistic in his insistence on writing only when there were certain objects on his writing desk. These included a French bronze of two fat toads fighting a duel with swords; one of them lunges forward and appears to be fatally piercing his adversary in the stomach. Another was a statuette of a dog-fancier with little dogs under his arms and pouring out of his pockets. And there was always a huge paper-knife, that he often held in his hand during his public readings. A small vase, ornamented with cowslips, would contain fresh flowers. Nearby was a register with his commitments for the week and month. Whenever he was in residence he had a flag hoisted at the top of the house.

Today the premises are usually closed to visitors. It has to be remembered that the house is the working environment of a school. Occasionally there are open days for Dickens enthusiasts but the school's privacy should be respected. Much can be seen and appreciated from the public highway. On the open days it is possible to explore the garden at the back. In it is a replica of the grave of Dick, the canary, a favourite of Dickens. Dick came from Broadstairs, lived to the age of fifteen years and used to be provided with a thimbleful of sherry at 11:00 every morning.

In the garden can also be found part of the balustrade of the medieval Rochester bridge, demolished in 1859. It was presented to Dickens who had it 'set up on the lawn behind the house. I have ordered a sundial for the top of it, and it will be a very good object indeed.'

To the west of the house were meadows. Each year Dickens collected hay from them, but they were also used for open air parties and gatherings for popular sports. In 1866 the meadow was filled with over 2,000 people attending sports and games.

I allowed the landlord of the Falstaff to have a drinking-booth on the ground. Not to seem to dictate or distrust, I gave all the prizes (about ten pounds in the aggregate) in money. The great mass of the crowd were labouring men of all kinds, soldiers, sailors, and navvies. They did not between half-past ten, when we began, and sunset, displace a rope or a stake; and they left every barrier and flag as neat as they found it. There was not a dispute and there was no drunkenness whatever ... Among other oddities we had a Hurdle Race for Strangers. One man (he came in second) ran 120 yards and leapt over ten hurdles, in twenty seconds, *with a pipe in his mouth, and smoking it all the time.* 'If it hadn't been for your pipe,' I said to him at the winning post, 'you would have been first.' 'I beg your pardon, Sir' he answered, 'but if it hadn't been for my pipe, I should have been nowhere.'

One area was set aside as a cricket ground. Although he was never a hearty sportsman, Dickens enjoyed cricket. If there was a deficit in the funds of the Higham Cricket Club at the end of the season he used to make it up. Indeed the last cheque he ever signed was for the Club. The Club used to play regularly in the meadow at the back of the house. Dickens stipulated that this privilege would be withdrawn if there were cases of drunkenness or bad language. He often hurried back to Gad's

Hill from London in order to attend a match and keep the score.

While the changes were being undertaken Dickens sometimes stayed at the Sir John Falstaff – and occasionally at Gravesend – so as to supervise the improvements and repairs on the spot. The inn went back centuries, though the building in Dickens's time – and in ours – dates probably from the eighteenth century. In the 1860s the landlord was a Mr Trood, a name suggestive of Drood. A few days after Dickens's death in 1870, a fan made a pilgrimage to Gad's Hill and called at the inn and shared his loss with the waiter.

'A great loss this of Mr Dickens,' said the pilgrim.

'A very great loss to us, sir,' replied the waiter, shaking his head; 'he had all his ale sent in from this house!'

When the Dickens family moved into Gad's Hill Place in the summer of 1857, it consisted of Catherine, his sister-in-law Georgina, his daughters, Mary (always known as Mamie), then 19 years old, and Catherine (Katey), aged 18; and his seven sons – Charley, 20, Walter, 16, Frank, 13, Alfred, 12, Sydney, 10, Henry (Harry), 8, and Edward (known as Plorn), 4. His wife, Catherine, only came to Gad's Hill once, in the summer of 1857. Georgina was taking over much of the household management as relations between Dickens and his wife were heading towards disaster and separation – this was the summer he met Ellen (Nelly) Ternan. After the separation Georgina stayed on with her brother-in-law, sharing the honours as hostess with the eldest daughter, Mamie. One of the merits of Georgina, in Dickens's eyes, was that she was one of the few people – and certainly the only woman – who could keep pace with him on his energetic walks.

One of the first of Dickens's guests at Gad's Hill Place was the Danish writer, Hans Christian Andersen. The stay was a disaster. He expected to be waited on in bed and demanded that he be shaved by Dickens's eldest son, Charley, to the latter's 'intense indignation'. Charley, who was no trained barber, declined the office. 'The whole day', Andersen recorded pitifully in his diary, 'I went with a great growth of beard'. Charley had spent time in Germany and knew the language but was unable to understand Andersen's German; his English was unintelligible and none of the family spoke Danish. He was quarrelsome, and could not keep up with his host as a walker. Dickens, normally most forbearing towards his guests, confided to Lady Burdett-Coutts, 'We are suffering very much from Andersen'. He was finally taken to Maidstone where he took a train to Folkestone, going from there back to Denmark. Such was relief of the family that Dickens had a placard placed on a table his guest had used, with the words, 'Hans Andersen slept in this room for five weeks which seemed to the family ages.' But not all the family, for the soon-to-be-dumped Mrs Dickens got on very well with him.

Charley was in awe of his father and used to address him as Sir. Other sons brought friends along from school. His son Alfred brought some of his mates who had been a bit anxious about meeting the great man, but were won over. 'By Jove, Dickens', one said to Alfred afterwards, 'your governor is a stunner and no mistake'. The sons joined him on outings. Sometimes they rowed him up the Medway from Rochester to Maidstone. At other times they strode with him, usually a pace or so behind. He seemed to need their company but he was often quite silent. Sometimes his lips would be at work as if he was composing speeches.

Dickens was a great host and within a few years there emerged a pattern in his hospitality. He would often meet his guests personally at Higham railway station and drive them in his pony-drawn 'jaunting car' – one of his ponies was called Newman Noggs, after the character in *Nicholas Nickleby*. On arrival at the house his guests were given a cider cup, a cooling drink with a mixture of cider, soda water, sherry, brandy, lemon-peel, sugar and ice, topped with a sprig of borage. Guest rooms were always comfortable, provided with a small library, warm fires and tea-making facilities. The Sir John Falstaff inn was used as an overflow for guests when all the bedrooms in the house were occupied. A buffet breakfast was provided – but Dickens would have got up early and regularly worked in the library on correspondence or on stories. He was not to be disturbed and the house was expected to be quiet. Guests had to amuse themselves. Lunch was served at 1:30 p.m., after which came a systematic programme of entertainment, with boisterous din and bustle. This might include energetic walks to Cobham Park, accompanied by his dogs, or to other villages around. Sometimes, with scrupulous attention to detail, Dickens would organise picnics. After leaving the picnic site, Dickens would ensure that no litter was left behind – in some ways he was a very modern man. Or Dickens might take guests in his barouche (a type of smart horse-drawn carriage) to look at Rochester Castle. This took up the time until dinner, a more formal occasion. Dickens used to provide his male guests with a button-hole, a scarlet geranium – his favourite flower. Dickens did not like the custom of ladies withdrawing after dinner; he would lead the way after only a few minutes to the drawing room. Some time might be spent with daughter Mamie and sister-in-law Georgina but then, if there were no party games, men withdrew to the billiard room to smoke, play cards or chat. Dickens himself went to bed at midnight, leaving one of his sons in charge to look after the guests and to 'see the gas out all right.'

There are many accounts of Gad's Hill hospitality. Not always did Dickens take centre stage. One visitor was the great violinist, Joseph Joachim, who played Tartini's *Devil's Sonata*. Dickens was overwhelmed by it.

Dickens was a genial and considerate host, and even turned tragedy into theatre. One of his dogs, an Irish mastiff called Sultan, was ferocious and usually had to be chained and muzzled. On one occasion a troop of soldiers was passing along the road. Sultan broke free of his chain and caused havoc in the ranks. He also killed and possibly ate a kitten. And he nearly swallowed Mrs Bouncer, a white Pomeranian dog belonging to Mamie. When he injured and terrified a little girl, his doom was sealed. George Dolby tells the story, quoting Dickens, how

> Sultan was sentenced to death and a procession was formed, consisting of some six or seven men and boys from the stables and garden, a wheelbarrow and a gun. The dog evidently thought, in the bloodthirstiness of his nature, of being let loose to join in the procession, that they were going to kill some one or something else; and it was only when he had gone half-way across the large field at the back of the house,

that his eye rested on the wheelbarrow with a gun in it. It seemed to strike him there was something wrong, and he at once became depressed, looking steadfastly at the gardener, and walked to his place of execution with his head down.

Arrived at the corner of the field farthest from the house, one of the boys threw a large stone to induce the dog to go after it, or to lead him to believe there was something in the hedge where it stuck. When Sultan's attention was thus diverted, two barrels were discharged into his heart, and he died without a struggle or a cry, deeply regretted by his loving master, who, be it said, was the only friend he had.

Another pet had a long posthumous existence at Gad's Hill. In the 1840s when he lived in Devonshire Terrace, Dickens had owned a pet raven, called Grip (the name also of Barnaby Rudge's bird). Grip poisoned himself with white lead, uttering as his dying words, 'Halloa, old girl!' Dickens had the bird stuffed and took him to his home in Tavistock Square and brought him to Gad's Hill Place. He was auctioned off with other effects after Dickens's death.

After the formal separation in the summer of 1858, Dickens's oldest son, Charley, chose to stay with his mother. Frank, Alfred and Sydney were, after the summer, sent to a boarding school in Boulogne. They did not come home for Christmas. It was no jolly family Christmas for the Dickens family.

It was clear that his second daughter, Katey, sided with her mother. She took the first opportunity to escape the household by marrying in 1860. She was wooed by Charles, artist brother of Wilkie Collins. Dickens was not happy about the marriage. Katey did not seem enthusiastic and there were suspicions that

Charles was homosexual. The marriage took place, however, in July 1860 at Higham church, two miles from Gad's Hill Place. The best man was the painter Holman Hunt. Dickens wrote afterwards that 'we had tried to keep it quiet here, but the church was filled with people, and the energetic blacksmith of the village had erected a triumphal arch in the court, and fired guns all night beforehand'. There were emotional strains, for the bride's mother was not invited – Dickens's hospitality did not extend to her – and Katey was in tears when the couple were seen off at Higham station, heading for Dover and a continental honeymoon. Later that evening, Dickens's other daughter, Mamie, found her father sobbing into Katey's bridal dress. 'But for me,' he said, 'Katey would not have left home'.

Two months later, in a further break with the past, Dickens organised a huge bonfire in the meadow at the back. Onto it he threw all the letters he had received. They included the letters from Catherine as well as from family friends and countless public figures and fans. Catherine kept the letters he had written to her as evidence 'that he loved me once'. After the archival holocaust, his sons roasted onions in the ashes as Dickens sighed, 'Would to God every letter I have ever written was on that pile.' Happily for posterity they were not, but were kept by their recipients and have been collected in twelve vast volumes, demonstrating what a stylish and brilliant correspondent he was.

The following year, 1861, Charley married a daughter of the publisher Frederick Evans. Charles Dickens had fallen out with Evans, disapproved of the marriage and did not attend the wedding ceremony. The quarrel with his son did not last and when a granddaughter was born, the family were regular visitors to Gad's Hill. The granddaughter, Mary Angela, called her grandfather Venerables or Wenerables.

In the years ahead the family was to become scattered. Walter, who had attended school at Wimbledon, took up a cadetship in an infantry division of the East India Company and set sail for India in the summer of 1861. Dickens was never to see him again, for he died in Calcutta in 1863. The third son, Frank, went out that autumn to join the Bengal Mounted Police and was savagely disappointed to arrive in Calcutta to learn of Walter's death. The fourth son, Sydney, left to join the navy. He incurred huge debts, which his father had to pay off, and Dickens was so cross that he refused to allow him to come to Gad's Hill. Another son, Alfred, also ran up debts. He failed to qualify to join the Royal Engineers, worked for a while in the City and then emigrated to Australia, where he was joined by the youngest son, Edward, known as Plorn. So Dickens never saw five of his seven sons after they took up their overseas careers.

Only the second youngest son, Henry, failed to disappoint his father. He was hard-working and, after schooling first in Boulogne, then at Rochester Grammar and finally at Wimbledon, won a scholarship in 1869 to Trinity Hall, Cambridge. He was overjoyed and went to Higham station to meet his father off the train from London. 'As he got out of the train', recalled Henry over half a century later, 'I told him the news. He said, "Capital! Capital!" – nothing more. Disappointed to find that he received the news apparently so lightly, I took my seat beside him in the pony carriage he was driving. Nothing more happened until we got half-way to Gad's Hill, when he broke down completely. Turning towards me with tears in his eyes and giving me a warm grip of the hand, he said, "God bless you, my boy, God bless you!'" Paradoxically, Henry succeeded in the one profession that his father had so consistently satirised – the law. There are as few good lawyers in Dickens's work as there are bad sailors. Henry went on to become a distinguished lawyer, a KC, a knight and the grandfather of the novelist Monica Dickens. He was the last of Dickens's children to die – in 1933.

At the time of Dickens's death only his sister-in-law Georgina and daughter Mamie were still at Gad's Hill Place. They were the keepers of Dickens's reputation and jointly edited the first collection of Dickens's letters. Georgina, the formidable Miss Hogarth, outlived her niece, Mamie, by over twenty years, dying in 1917 at the age of ninety.

Dickens became a much-loved celebrity in his last years at Gad's Hill. He was an active benefactor of the village. The parish church was two miles from Gad's Hill and he was an occasional worshipper there. Between the railway station and Gad's Hill was Upper Higham, and a new church was built there in 1860. Dickens had a pew there in the chancel.

In May 1868 he returned to Gad's Hill after six months in the United States. He had been exhausted by the tour, and had been too unwell to travel to Chicago and the mid-West. But the return sea voyage had restored his vigour. It was expected that he would arrive at Higham Station. The villagers planned to meet him there and take the horse out of the carriage and drag him up the one and a quarter miles to his home. Mamie and Miss Hogarth heard about this, telegraphed Dickens and arranged for his carriage to meet him at Gravesend. The villagers, in the words of his readings manager, George Dolby, 'turned out on foot, and in their market carts and gigs; and escorting Mr Dickens on the road, kept on giving him shouts of welcome, the houses along the road being decorated with flags. His own servants wanted to ring the alarm bell in the little belfry at the top of the house ...'

Dickens was not a well man in his last years. He was easily tired and was periodically lame. He rented a flat at Hyde Park Place for the sake of his unmarried daughter, Mamie, and also retained his bachelor pad off the Strand. He was also seeing Nelly Ternan at the house he acquired for her at Windsor Lodge, Peckham. He came down to Gad's Hill Place as often as he could, where he was working on *The Mystery of Edwin Drood*. The illustrator of this last novel was Luke Fildes, who would come to Gad's Hill to check on details. Dickens used to act out the scenes he wanted illustrated.

He had a final season of readings in the early months of 1870, ultimately bidding his audience at St James's Hall in London 'a heartfelt, grateful, respectful, and affectionate farewell'. One day at Gad's Hill his son, Harry, heard the awful din of what seemed to be a very violent domestic row going on in the garden. At first he thought it was tramps. But the row went on with increased fury. He went outside and found his father rehearsing for 'Sikes and Nancy', reading from *Oliver Twist*. By all accounts it was an intense act, emotionally and physically.

During his last month Dickens was also, typically, supervising the building of a new conservatory. This was the last of many improvements to the house. When Gad's Hill Place was sold after his death, it sold – partly because of the improvements, partly because of the association – at four times the price he had paid for it.

There were many claims on his time, social and professional, in London. He returned to Gad's Hill at the beginning of June 1870. On Sunday evening, 5 June, his daughter, Katey, sought his advice on a personal matter. Her artist husband was ailing and they were in need of money. She wanted to take up acting professionally. Sitting in the new conservatory he advised strongly against it. There were people in the theatre, he said, 'who would make your hair stand on end'. (Well, he should know.) When she retired to bed – it was well after 11:00 p.m. – he called her back and talked of his plans, and his writing of *The Mystery of Edwin Drood*, 'if, please God, I live to finish it. I say *if* because you know, my dear child, I have not been strong lately'. He went on to regret that he had not 'been a better father – a better man'. It was 3:00 a.m. before they went to bed.

Next morning, Monday, Dickens was up early. He went to the chalet to work on the novel. Katey and Mamie were due to go to London. Unusually Katey went through the tunnel to say goodbye. 'His head was bent low over his work', she recalled, 'and he turned an eager and rather flushed face towards me as I entered. On ordinary occasions he would just have raised his cheek for my kiss, saying a few words, perhaps in "the little language" that he had been accustomed to use when we were children; but on this morning, when he saw me, he pushed his chair from the writing-table, opened his arms, and took me into them.' She never saw him conscious again.

On the Monday afternoon he was fit enough to walk with his dogs into Rochester and back. The next day, Tuesday, he wrote more in the chalet and in the afternoon was driven with Georgina into Cobham, where he dismissed the carriage and walked the three or four miles back to Gad's Hill.

On Wednesday, 8 June, he was in good spirits, worked on the novel in the morning, crossed under the road for lunch, and after a cigar, returned, unusually to write more in the afternoon. He wrote several pages of *The Mystery of Edwin Drood*, including the beautiful loving lines on the city of Rochester that are the introduction of the next section of this book. He returned to the house, and wrote a couple of letters. The only member of the family present, Georgina, noticed that he seemed changed and asked him if he was ill. 'Yes, very ill', he answered. 'I have been very ill for the last hour.' He talked of going up to London after dinner and then had a seizure. Georgina urged him to lie down. 'Yes', he said, 'on the ground.' These were his last words. He collapsed onto the floor. Georgina sent for Dr Steele, from Strood, who had regularly treated Dickens. Dickens was eased onto a couch, unconscious and wrapped up. Charley and the daughters were summoned back from London and his London doctor, Frank Beard, sent for. He and the daughters arrived and, with Georgina, held vigil through the night.

The following morning, Thursday 9 June, Charley arrived, and Dr Steele came up again from Rochester. Georgina arranged for Ellen Ternan to come. She reached Gad's Hill Place in the afternoon. Dickens never recovered consciousness. He died shortly after 6:00 p.m. the same day in the drawing room, the ground floor room which is on the left as you face the front door. It was the fifth anniversary of the railway accident at Staplehurst when he and Nelly had nearly been killed together. He was fifty-eight.

In due course a death mask was made. The painter, John Millais, came to Gad's Hill and made a drawing of the face of the dead man. The body was placed in an oak coffin adorned with scarlet geraniums. In accordance with his instructions, his horse was shot. He had wanted to be buried locally, at Shorne Church perhaps, or at Rochester cathedral, but a national campaign called for burial in Westminster Abbey. Dickens hated the rituals of death and wanted no great funeral. So on Tuesday morning early the coffin was taken to Higham station, and on to Charing Cross. And then to Poet's Corner.

It has been argued that Dickens worked himself to death, dying prematurely. The readings, and especially the American tour of 1867–68, had exhausted him and ruined his health. His friend and first major biographer, John Forster, had advised against the readings and especially the American tour. But it could be that the readings actually kept him going.

His strenuous walking aside, Dickens was never a healthy man. He describes himself as having been 'puny' as a child in Chatham, shunning hearty games. Throughout his life he suffered from streaming head colds; one such cold had prevented him from attending a theatre audition when he was twenty. And although he was never the worse for it, he was a heavy drinker all his life and a smoker.

Dickens also did not come from a long-living family. His father died at sixty-six and his mother at seventy-four, but of his siblings who survived infancy, three of his four brothers died in their thirties and one in his forties; only one sister, Letitia, lived into her seventies. There is a similar pattern with his own children. Nine (out of ten) survived infancy. Only four lived to a greater age than Dickens was when he died. Katey and Harry lived to the ages of eighty-nine and eighty-four respectively, but two of the other children died in their twenties and one in his forties. The death of Charles Dickens at fifty-eight was not an early death by the standards of his own family.

His eldest son, Charley, moved into Gad's Hill Place. He also inherited his father's role as editor/'conductor' of *All the Year Round*. Many of his father's effects were sold later in 1870. These included hundreds of bottles of wine, spirits and liqueurs. While Charley and his family lived in the house, Dickens's widow was often a visitor and used to come for Christmas. After Dickens's death, the family reunited around Mrs Dickens who, from being the novelist's discarded wife, became the widow of a national treasure, receiving a message of condolence from Queen Victoria.

Charley sold the house in 1879. It had several owners in the following decades. One of them had the offer from a potential American purchaser of £10,000 for the house, which he wanted to transfer – like London Bridge – to the United States. In 1924 the house became Gad's Hill School, a successful independent school. A great-great-grand-daughter of the novelist is a former pupil and a current member of the board of governors.

The Medway Towns

Rochester and Strood

A brilliant morning shines on the old city. Its antiquities and ruins are surprisingly beautiful, with the lusty ivy gleaming in the sun, and the rich trees waving in the balmy air. Changes of glorious light from moving boughs, songs of birds, scents from gardens, woods, and fields – or rather, from the one great garden of the whole cultivated island in its yielding time – penetrate into the Cathedral, subdue its earthy odour, and preach the Resurrection and the Life. The cold stone tombs of centuries ago grow warm, and flecks of brightness dart into the sternest marble corners of the building, fluttering there like wings.

THESE MOVING WORDS were among the last that Charles Dickens wrote. They were penned in his chalet on Wednesday 8 June. He worked all day and was taken ill in the early evening and died the following afternoon. To the end there was no flagging of his literary power, as he conjured up with deftly crafted phrases his loving perception of the city of Rochester.

Rochester features in his first novel, *The Pickwick Papers*, and as Cloisterham in his last, *The Mystery of Edwin Drood*. It plays a major part in *Great Expectations* as the market town and there is a passing reference to it in *David Copperfield*. As Great Winglebury it features in *Sketches by Boz*. The Medway Towns – Rochester and Chatham primarily, but also the other towns of Strood, Gillingham and Brompton – were as important in Dickens's life and work as London. He had spent magical childhood years in Chatham, was stirred by the antiquities of the old cathedral city of Rochester and, after he moved to Gad's Hill in 1857, was fond of walking or riding the two miles or so into the city. He loved to show Rochester off to visitors. There he was a familiar figure, but not always correctly identified. One year before he died his American friend, James T. Fields, was staying at Gad's Hill. Fields and Dickens were in Rochester together and the American was mistaken for the Englishman. Dickens encouraged the deception and handed over a parcel, saying loudly, 'Here you are, Dickens, take charge of this for me.'

The two main Medway towns, Rochester and Chatham, have seen better days. Rochester was a Roman city and its cathedral and castle testify to its importance in early medieval times. At that time the first bridge over the Medway was built, making the city a major land transit stop between the capital, Canterbury and Dover, and the continent. Since the nineteenth century, however, there has been a steady decline. The main trans-Kent railway routes, both in the nineteenth and the twenty-first century, have bypassed the Medway towns, which have also been marginalised by the motorways.

An industrial zone on the Medway, south of the bridge at Rochester, produced many of the world's cement mixers and steam traction engines for much of the twentieth century. The towns became a major commuting region and benefitted from tourism. Chatham in particular once prospered as a naval and military base, with a major shipyard and associated trades. But over the last century they have seen a gentle and dignified decline. Twenty-first century disparities of wealth are apparent in the contrast between the smart craft in the marinas and the rows of depressed terrace housing throughout the Medway towns.

Mr Micawber in *David Copperfield* contemplated a career in the Medway Coal Trade. 'My opinion of the coal trade on that river,' declared Mrs Micawber, 'is, that it may require talent, but that it certainly requires capital. Talent, Mr Micawber has; capital, Mr Micawber has not.' The Kentish coalfields are well to the south and east of the Medway and so, despite his talent, even if Mr Micawber had been in possession of capital, it was unlikely that he would have prospered.

For Mr Pickwick, the 'chief productions of these towns ... appear to be soldiers, sailors, Jews, chalk, shrimps, officers, and dockyard men. The commodities chiefly exposed for sale in the public streets are marine stores, hardbake, apples, flat-fish, and oysters.'

In the 1820s, the time of Mr Pickwick and when the young Charles Dickens was living locally, the Medway towns had a well-established Jewish community. It was mainly Sephardic and had commercial connections with the Low Countries and the Baltic. Often Jews acted as naval agents, drawing a profit from the prize money when ships captured during the wars were sold off. After the Napoleonic Wars many became chandlers or military tailors.

A few years earlier, Dickens wrote a thumbnail sketch of the town, disguised as Great Winglebury, in *Sketches by Boz*. The town, he wrote in Jinglesque prose, 'has a long straggling quiet High Street, with a great black and white clock at a small red Town Hall, half way up – a market place – a cage – an assembly room – a church – a bridge – a chapel – a theatre – a library – an inn – a pump – and a post office.' He also places the town 'exactly forty-two miles and three-quarters from Hyde Park Corner'. (Rochester is under thirty miles from the City of London – just over thirty from Hyde Park Corner.)

The mostly pedestrianised High Street that runs from Rochester Bridge to Star Hill is the spine of Dickensian Rochester. To the west of the bridge is the town of Strood. From there, the road to Gravesend climbs up to Gad's Hill. In the town on the right of the road was the old inn Crispin and Crispianus. This was severely damaged by fire in 2011 and is currently boarded up. There used to be a Dickens Room, commemorating the fact that this was a favourite watering hole for Dickens on his walks into the Medway Towns. He used to drop in for a glass of sixpenny ale, or some cold brandy and water. It was noted that he rarely spoke to anyone but seemed to survey the scene, taking everything in. He had his favourite seat in a corner near the fireplace. The landlady recalled one occasion when Dickens called in during a thunderstorm. He saw a lady with a baby in the rain outside and asked the landlady to call her in and give her some brandy. She drank the brandy and Dickens gave her a shilling, telling the landlady, 'Now she will go on her way rejoicing.'

Today there are actually four parallel bridges over the River Medway – two carrying lanes of the A2 road, one carrying the railway and one carrying service pipes and cables. Until 1856 a medieval bridge was in use. This was the bridge on which

Mr Pickwick strolled, 'contemplating nature, and waiting for breakfast ... On either side the banks of the Medway, covered with cornfields and pastures, stretched away as far as the eye could see, presenting a rich and varied landscape, rendered more beautiful by the changing shadows which passed swiftly across it, as the thin and half-formed clouds skimmed away in the light of the morning sun.' No cornfields or pastures flank the river today. Nor do we see a rich and varied landscape: all is built over. On another occasion Mr Pickwick was on the bridge and shunned a 'dismal' man, whom he thought might tip himself – taking Mr Pickwick with him – into the river. This was the bridge David Copperfield would have crossed over as a boy, 'as evening closes in ... footsore and tired'. It was also the bridge across which Pip, in his prosperity, was pursued with taunts by Trabb's boy in *Great Expectations*.

The medieval bridge was demolished by the Royal Engineers in 1856. Parts of the balustrade were recycled and placed on the esplanade to the south, and one part of the bridge was presented to Dickens, who had just bought Gad's Hill Place. He used it as the base of a sundial. A new road bridge was constructed and a year later a railway bridge built. The second road bridge was built in 1970.

The castle dominates the eastern side of the city of Rochester today, as it did in the time of Mr Pickwick:

'Magnificent ruin,' said Mr Snodgrass with all the poetic fervour that distinguished him ...

'What a sight for the antiquarian,' were the words which fell from Mr Pickwick's mouth, as he applied his telescope to his eye.

'Ah! Fine place,' said the stranger [the plausible fraud-ster, Alfred Jingle], 'glorious pile, frowning walls – tottering arches ...'

The castle is no more than a backdrop to Dickens's fiction, as to the events of *The Mystery of Edwin Drood*. The castle was in private hands until the nineteenth century, a crumbling ruin, or, as Dickens wrote in *The Pickwick Papers*, 'Its towers roofless, and its massive walls crumbling away, but telling us proudly of its own might and strength, as when, seven hundred years ago, it rang with the clash of arms, or resounded with the noise of feasting and revelry.'

In the early years of the nineteenth century there were pro-posals for turning the castle into barracks. Access was forbid-den. In 1842 Dickens, fresh from his American tour, brought Henry Wadsworth Longfellow and his future biographer, John Forster, to Rochester. Forster recalled how they con-fronted 'one of those prohibitions which are the wonder of visitors and the shame of Englishmen ... [We] overleapt gates and barriers, and setting at defiance repeated threats of all the terrors of the law coarsely expressed to us by the custodian of the place, explored minutely the castle ruins.'

The corporation of the City of Rochester acquired the free-hold of the castle (for £6,572) in 1884. Today it is cared for by English Heritage.

The other great medieval building that has dominated the geography and history of the city for nearly a millennium is the Cathedral Church of Christ and the Blessed Virgin Mary.

Old Cathedral too [Mr Jingle again], earthy smell

– pilgrims' feet worn away the old steps – little Saxon doors
– confessionals like money-takers' boxes at theatres – queer
customers those monks – Popes, and Lord Treasurers, and
all sorts of old fellows, with great red faces, and broken
noses, turning up every day – buff jerkins too – matchlocks
– sarcophagus – fine place – old legends too – strange
stories: capital.

The cathedral, or 'Kinfreederel' as the stone-throwing
urchin, Deputy, calls it in *The Mystery of Edwin Drood*, is the
background for that novel.

The outer buildings of the cathedral precincts also feature in
much of the novel. When the London lawyer comes to Rochester, he too is impressed. "'Dear me," said Mr Grewgious,' who
otherwise presents himself as an 'Angular' man without imagination or poetry, 'peeping in [the cathedral]. "It's like looking
down the throat of Old Time.'"

Inside the cathedral Dickens is commemorated by a brass
tablet on the wall of the south transept 'to connect his memory
with the scenes in which his earliest and his latest years were
passed and with the associations of Rochester Cathedral and
its neighbourhood which extended over all his life.' Nearby,
another tablet from an earlier century commemorates Richard
Watts, founder of the charitable house for the relief of poor
travellers.

Dickens's description of the architecture of the cathedral
in *The Mystery of Edwin Drood* is literal. Beyond describing the picturesque and sometimes giving buildings human
or animal characteristics, we do not go to Dickens for great
architectural insights. He wrote of 'the low arched Cathedral

door' at the west front, 'the massive grey square tower' and 'the rugged steps' leading down to the crypt, with its 'groined windows, bare of glass' and 'heavy pillars which support the roof' and 'engender masses of black shade.' He is far more eloquent when describing music and sounds associated with the building. In *Great Expectations* the only reference to Rochester Cathedral is when Pip reflects on how Estella has slipped out of his hands:

> The best light of the day was gone when I passed along the quiet echoing courts behind the High Street. The nooks of ruin where the old monks had once had their refectories and gardens, and where the strong walls were now pressed into the humble sheds and stables, were almost as silent as their graves. The cathedral chimes had at once a sadder and a more remote sound to me, as I hurried on avoiding observation, than they had ever had before; so, the swell of the old organ was borne to my ears like funeral music; and the rooks, as they hovered about the grey tower and swung in the bare trees of the priory-garden, seemed to call to me that the place was changed, and that Estella was gone out of it for ever.

To the south of the cathedral is Minor Canons Row, a terrace of eighteenth-century houses. Here in *The Mystery of Edwin Drood* lived the Reverend Mr Crisparkle and his mother. Dickens describes how 'the houses had little porches over the doors, like sounding-boards over old pulpits'. They still do. By one of the doors is a plaque, not to the Crisparkles but to the actors Sybil and Russell Thorndike, who spent some of their childhood in the tied cottage allotted to their father, who was a canon of the cathedral.

To the west of Minor Canon Row is the garden known as The Vines, called in *The Mystery of Edwin Drood* 'the Monks' Vineyard'. Edwin and his affianced Rosa Bud used to stroll in these gardens. These were the vineyards, just outside the walls of the city, of the medieval abbey connected to the cathedral. On the street to the west of the gardens is Restoration House, a massive construction which the perceptive observer will see was originally two houses. There is little architectural unity and no symmetry in the building, which was constructed in the sixteenth century but probably on medieval foundations. The two houses were joined up in the middle of the following century. In 1660 it was occupied by a disillusioned Cromwellian soldier, Colonel Gibbon, though owned by a Royalist, Francis Clerke. Gibbon hosted King Charles II on his return from eleven years' exile during the Commonwealth period. Hence the name of Restoration House. Another visitor to the house in the reign of King Charles II was the diarist, Samuel Pepys. He was visiting the Medway towns in his capacity as an official (like Dickens's own father) of the Royal Navy. He noted that the house was a pretty seat, with a cherry garden where he 'met with a young, plain, silly shopkeeper and his wife, a pretty young woman, and I did kiss her.'

In 1986 the television comedian, Rod Hull, famous for his puppet, an aggressive emu, bought the house for £270,000. Hull was a local lad, having been born on the Isle of Sheppey. He spent half a million on the house but went bankrupt, and the house was repossessed.

Dickens made the house the model for Miss Havisham's

house in *Great Expectations*: a house 'of old brick, and dismal, and had a great many iron bars to it. Some of the windows had been walled up; of those that remained, all the lower were rustily barred. There was a courtyard in front, and that was barred; so, we had to wait, after ringing the bell, until some one should come to open it.'

On his last visit to Rochester, Dickens was seen leaning against the railings opposite Restoration House, gazing at the building. It is believed that if he had been able to continue writing *The Mystery of Edwin Drood*, the building may have made an appearance in that book.

In *Great Expectations* Miss Havisham's house is called Satis House. There is a Satis House on Boley Hill to the south-east of the cathedral. It was the home of Richard Watts, sixteenth-century philanthropist and Member of Parliament for Rochester. Watts entertained his sovereign, Queen Elizabeth I, in Rochester. She declared her *satis*faction with his hospitality and the name reflects the Queen's content.

Restoration House is today privately owned, but the house and gardens are open to the public some days during the summer.

Let us return to Rochester Bridge and walk through the city, along the High Street.

Dickens first knew the street between the ages of seven and eleven when he lived at Chatham. In middle age he returned to live at Gad's Hill and wrote about the Medway towns in an essay, 'Dullborough Town', published in *All the Year Round* in 1860. As he perceived it, during the intervening thirty-six years 'the town had shrunk fearfully. I had entertained the impression that the High Street was at least as wide as Regent-street,

London, or the Italian Boulevard at Paris. I found it little better than a lane'.

'The silent High Street,' Dickens wrote in his Christmas story 'The Seven Poor Travellers', 'is full of gables, with old beams and timbers carved into strange faces. It is oddly garnished with a queer old clock that projects over the pavement out of a grave red brick building, as if Time carried on business there, and hung out his sign.'

The projecting clock is on the Corn Exchange on the left (northern) side of the road. In his 1860 essay he recalled his childhood impressions of that clock, which he had

supposed to be the finest clock in the world: whereas it now turned out to be as inexpressive, moon-faced, and weak a clock as ever I saw. It belonged to a Town Hall, where I had seen an Indian (who I now suppose wasn't an Indian) swallow a sword (which I now suppose he didn't.) The edifice had appeared to me in those days so glorious a structure, that I had set it up in mind as the model on which the Genie of the Lamp built the palace for Aladdin.

But before we reach the Corn Exchange there are two other major buildings of Dickensian interest. On the right is the Bull Inn, or more correctly, the Royal Victoria and Bull. This historic inn is on a medieval site, though the present building dates from the late eighteenth century.

This was the Winglebury Arms in *Sketches by Boz* and the place where the Pickwickians stayed on their visit to Rochester. Mr Jingle stayed elsewhere but he did commend the Bull as a 'nice house – good beds'.

Today the Royal Victoria and Bull hotel is largely closed for refurbishment, but in *Sketches by Boz*, the inn had 'a great, wide rambling staircase, three stairs and a landing – four stairs and another landing – one step and another landing – half-a-dozen stairs and another landing – and so on – [that] conducts to galleries of bedrooms, and labyrinths of sitting-rooms ...' The staircase is a rectangular spiral but there are further narrower staircases leading to galleries of rooms. The staircase is where Jingle coolly insulted Dr Slammer in *The Pickwick Papers*. Those who stay at the hotel will not have great difficulty in visualising the hotel that Mr Pickwick stayed at.

'Devil of a mess on the staircase, waiter,' said the stranger. 'Forms going up – carpenters going down – lamps, glasses, harps. What's going forward?'

'Ball, Sir,' said the waiter.

Today on the staircase and on the landing are portraits and paintings of variable quality. The hotel's heyday is long past to judge from photographs of former patrons of the hotel hanging on the landing walls – they include Edward Heath and Ernest Marples.

To the left at the top of the stairs is the ballroom, the scene of the ball attended by Mr Jingle (in Mr Winkle's borrowed clothes) and Mr Tupman.

It was a long room, with crimson-covered benches, and wax candles in glass chandeliers. The musicians were securely confined in an elevated den, and quadrilles were being

systematically got through by two or three sets of dancers.
Two card tables were made up in the adjoining card-room,
and two pairs of old ladies, and a corresponding number of
stout gentlemen, were executing whist therein.

On my visit to the room I found it being used as a store but it
was possible to envisage it as Dickens described it in *The Pickwick Papers* – including the 'elevated den', a small overhanging
minstrels' gallery.

It is claimed that Mr Pickwick – and Charles Dickens
himself – occupied room number 17.

The inn also served as The Blue Boar in *Great Expectations*. After Pip received the twenty-five guineas from Miss
Havisham so he could be formally apprenticed to his brother-
in-law Joe, Pip's sister insisted that 'nothing would serve her
but we must have a dinner out of that windfall at the Blue
Boar.' This was held, presumably, at one of the sitting-rooms
upstairs for rather 'late in the evening Mr Wopsle gave us Collins's ode, and threw his blood-stain'd sword in thunder down,
with such effect that a waiter came in and said, "The Com-
mercials underneath send up their compliments, and it wasn't
the Tumblers' Arms"'.

The management of the Blue Boar treated Pip in accordance with his presumed fortunes. When he returned, knowing
that Miss Havisham had not been his benefactor,

> I found the Blue Boar in possession of the intelligence, and
> I found that it made a great change in the Boar's demean-
> our. Whereas the Boar had cultivated my good opinion
> with warm assiduity when I was coming into prosperity,

the Boar was exceedingly cool on the subject now that I was going out of property.

It was evening when I arrived, much fatigued by the journey I had so often made so easily. The Boar could not put me in my usual bedroom, which was engaged (probably by some one who had expectations), and could only assign me a very indifferent chamber among the pigeons and post-chaises up the yard.

The second of the buildings of Dickensian interest is the Guildhall. It stands opposite the Royal Victoria and Bull and was built at the end of the seventeenth century as the headquarters of the city council, its courthouse and gaol. The principal room is still known as the Court Hall. Here, in *Great Expectations*, Pip was ceremoniously bound to Joe as his apprentice.

The Hall was a queer place, I thought, with higher pews in it than a church – and with people hanging over the pews looking on – and with mighty Justices (one with a powdered head) leaning back in chairs, with folded arms, or taking snuff, or going to sleep, or writing, or reading the newspapers – and with some shining black portraits on the walls, which my unartistic eye regarded as a composition of hardbake and sticking-plaster. Here, in a corner, my indentures were duly signed and attested, and I was 'bound'.

The high pews have gone, but much has not changed. The portraits include those of King William, Queen Anne and Sir Cloudesley Shovell – admiral and MP for Rochester. There was formerly a market under the arches below and the building was the seat for local government until 1974. Today it is an excellent (free) museum, with a couple of floors devoted to the prison hulks that were based in the Medway estuary until the middle of the nineteenth century.

Proceeding eastwards – past two second-hand bookshops – we pass the Corn Exchange with the clock described in 'Dullborough Town' – though Dickens placed the clock on the 'town hall'.

A little further on the right is a fifteenth-century gateway surmounted by an eighteenth-century upper storey. It led into the monastery attached to the cathedral. It is described in *The Mystery of Edwin Drood*:

> They all three looked towards an old stone gatehouse crossing the Close, with an arched thoroughfare passing beneath it. Through its latticed window, a fire shines out upon the fast-darkening scene, involving in shadow the pendent masses of ivy and creeper covering the building's front.

John Jasper lived in the gatehouse – 'my bachelor gatehouse' – then known as Chertsey's Gate but now better known as Jasper's Gate. Dickens describes the gateway as a 'lighthouse on the margin of the tide of busy life'. Next door lived the cathedral verger, Mr Tope, whose wife looked after John Jasper; the two households were interconnected. Today a Topes' restaurant occupies the old house.

Continuing eastward, just past the Information Centre, we come to Richard Watts's Charity. His monument is in the cathedral but the plaque on the wall of this building indicates that it was an endowed resort for 'six poor travellers' who could stay the night – one night only – and be given four pence when they left. Dickens visited the house in 1854 with Wilkie Collins. 'I found it to be a clean white house, of a staid and venerable air, with the quaint old door ... choice little latticed windows, and a roof of three gables.' He used the experience of the visit for his Christmas story later that year, 'The Seven Poor Travellers'. Dickens himself was the seventh – Collins was overlooked.

I found the party to be thus composed. Firstly, myself. Secondly, a very decent man indeed, with his right arm in a sling, who had a certain clean, agreeable smell of wood about him, from which I judged him to have something to do with shipbuilding. Thirdly, a little sailor-boy, a mere child, with a profusion of rich dark brown hair, and deep womanly-looking eyes. Fourthly, a shabby-genteel personage in a threadbare black suit, and apparently in very bad circumstances, with a dry, suspicious look; the absent buttons on his waistcoat eked out with red tape; and a bundle of extraordinarily tattered papers sticking out of an inner breast-pocket. Fifthly, a foreigner by birth, but an Englishman in speech, who carried his pipe in the band of his hat, and lost no time in telling me, in an easy, simple, engaging way, that he was a watchmaker from Geneva, and travelled all about the Continent, mostly on foot, working as a journeyman, and seeing new countries – possibly (I thought) also smuggling a watch or so, now and then. Sixthly, a little widow, who had been very pretty and was still very young, but whose beauty had been wrecked in some great misfortune, and whose manner was remarkably

timid, scared, and solitary. Seventhly and lastly, A Traveller
of a kind familiar to my boyhood, but now almost obso-
lete, – a Book-Peddler, who had a quantity of pamphlets
and Numbers with him, and who presently boasted that he
could repeat more verses in an evening than he could sell in
a twelvemonth.

Dickens's visit and story recorded the last years of the
charity that dated back to the sixteenth century. By the middle
of the nineteenth century the charity had accumulated a lot of
money. In the 1850s it was reorganised by the Trustees; the rest
house for travellers continued with a master and matron, but
£4,000 was put aside for the construction of almshouses on
the Maidstone Road, built in a Jacobean style – they can still
be seen. Public baths were built and apprenticeships provided
for the deserving poor. Many of the functions of the charity
have been taken over by the Welfare State but Watts's charitable work still continues with support for specific assistance in
local hospitals and with apprenticeships and financial support
for students.

Walking further east we pass the site of the Roman and
medieval walls. A stretch and a corner bastion can be seen to
the north. Once we are beyond the walled city, buildings that
date back to the Middle Ages are larger and more expansive.
To the left is Eastgate House. A massive Elizabethan building,
it is currently used for exhibitions and weddings. It was the
model for the Nuns' House in *The Mystery of Edwin Drood*
and was described as 'a venerable brick edifice, whose present
appellation is doubtless derived from the legend of its con-
ventual uses'. Here Rosa Bud went to the school run by Miss

Twinkleton (a name curiously like Miss Pinkerton, whose Academy is the scene of the first chapter of Thackeray's *Vanity Fair*). Dickens probably used the building as the model for another girls' school, Westgate House in *The Pickwick Papers*. Here Mr Pickwick scaled the wall in his attempt to entrap Captain FitzMarshall, aka Mr Jingle.

In the garden of Eastgate House is the chalet that was given to Dickens by Charles Fechter, and originally erected in the shrubbery across the road from Gad's Hill Place. 'In the summer', he wrote to John Forster, '(supposing it not to be blown away in the spring) the upper room will make a charming study'. There are two rooms, one above the other, each about sixteen feet square. There was an outside staircase, and Dickens had mirrors fitted into the upper room. He installed a small table and a sloping desktop, coach and chairs. It became his favourite place of work in summer months. He was cut off from the house. 'I used to hear what sounded like someone making a speech', one young gardener recalled years later. 'I wondered what it was at first, and then I found out. It was Mr Dickens composing his writing out loud.'

It was here in the chalet that Dickens wrote the last chapter of *Edwin Drood*, just before his fatal stroke. After his death, the chalet was moved to Crystal Palace for a year, and then found a home in the terrace garden at the back of Cobham Hall. It stayed there until 1961 when it was restored and erected in the gardens of Eastgate House. At present it is in need of repair. Rotten wood needs to be replaced. It is hoped that with funding raised by the local Dickens Fellowship and support from the National Lottery, the chalet will be fully restored. Part of the £23,000 raised by the Fellowship was the result of a raffle, the prize for which was an authenticated strand of Dickens's hair.

Diagonally opposite Eastgate House is 150–154 High Street. This was the home of Mr Sapsea in *The Mystery of Edwin Drood*. It is a shambling construction of three storeys, with shops on the ground floor. In the novel it is described as 'irregularly modernised here and there, as steady deteriorating generations found, more and more, that they preferred air and light to Fever and Plague'. The house is also considered to be where Mr Pumblechook in *Great Expectations* had his corn seed shop and residence, where Pip spent the night before setting off for London for the first time. He was 'sent straight to bed in an attic with a sloping roof, which was so low in the corner where the bedstead was, that I calculated the tiles as being within a foot of my eyebrows.'

The pedestrianised High Street ends at the junction with Star Hill. A few yards up Star Hill on the right are the Royal Function Rooms. They occupy a building constructed in the 1880s for the Conservative Club, as is clear from relief lettering beneath the gables. A plaque records that this was the site of the Rochester Theatre. Built in 1791, it was where Dickens, as a child, was taken to see the clown, Grimaldi, whose memoirs he was later to edit for publication. Here was born his passion for the theatre and 'a strong veneration for Clowns'. The acting was often ham and the sets amateurish, but this theatre moulded his sense of history and nurtured his love of Shakespeare.

Richard the Third, in a very uncomfortable cloak, had first appeared to me there, and had made my heart leap with terror by backing up against the stage-box in which I was posted, while struggling for life against the virtuous Richmond. It was within these walls that I had learnt as from a page of English history, how that wicked King slept in wartime on a sofa much too short for him, and how fearfully his conscience troubled his boots.

One story he remembered for the rest of his life was about an actor who completely forgot his lines at this theatre. He could neither hear the prompter nor attract his attention. But he had resource and strode off the stage with the words, 'I will return anon'; he left to refresh his memory from the script.

It was at the Rochester Theatre that Mr Jingle in *The Pickwick Papers* was engaged to play, co-starring with a 'rum fellow', as Jingle said, '– does the heavy business – no actor – strange man – all sorts of miseries – dismal Jemmy, we call him on the circuit'. One of Dr Slammer's companions recognised Jingle as having acted at the theatre, and as a strolling player he was not socially significant enough to be a partner in a duel.

Dickens returned to this theatre in 1860 but found it in 'a bad and declining way. A dealer in wine and bottled beer had already squeezed his trade into the box-office, and the theatrical money was taken – when it came – in a kind of meat-safe in the passage.' The theatre also appears in *The Mystery of Edwin Drood*: 'A new grand comic Christmas pantomime is to be produced at the Theatre: the latter heralded by the portrait of Signor Jacksonini the clown, saying, "How do you do to-morrow?"'

Another Dickensian theatrical connection with the Medway towns is in the history of the family of his mistress, Nelly Ternan. Nelly's parents met in Rochester. Her father, William, had been an actor in Rochester, and was also a trader. William met Frances (Fanny), also an actor, through the theatre in the town, and, although they toured as an acting family, Nelly herself was born in a small house on the Maidstone Road in March 1839 – in the same year as Dickens's second daughter, Katey. (Oddly enough, just as Nelly was born about three miles from where Dickens died, so she died in Southsea about three miles from where Dickens was born. Even more oddly, she is buried in Highland Road cemetery in Portsmouth, a hundred yards or so from the grave of Maria Beadnell, Dickens's first love. Such a coincidence would stretch credulity if it appeared in fiction.)

Chatham

> ... a mere dream of chalk, and drawbridges, and mastless ships in a muddy river, roofed like Noah's arks ...

These were David Copperfield's impressions of Chatham when he walked from London to Dover in search of his great-aunt Betsey Trotwood. He had walked twenty-three miles from Blackheath and had just been swindled into selling his remaining disposable clothes in order to buy some food.

Mr Jingle in *The Pickwick Papers* summarised the town in a similar pithy way:

> ... Queer place – Dock-yard people of upper rank don't know people of lower rank – Dock-yard people of lower rank don't know small gentry – small gentry don't know tradespeople – Commissioner don't know anybody.

Chatham was home to Charles Dickens for seven years from 1816, when he was four, until the summer of 1823. Positive impressions of the town remained with him for the rest of his life. It was, in the words of his friend and biographer, John Forster, 'the birthplace of his fancy'. If he had any home town, it was Chatham. His father worked at the dockyard, dealing with pay for the Navy; the Naval Pay Office where he worked dates from 1808, and survives, a handsome Georgian building. A plaque records the fact that John Dickens worked here. Added to it is another plaque noting that a great-grandson of Charles Dickens, Captain P. G. C. Dickens, was captain of the Dockyard in 1963. The town of Chatham, its sailors and the neighbourhood, all appear in his work. The young Dickens left the town by stagecoach and returned by train.

> The coach that had carried me away, was melodiously called Timpson's Blue-Eyed Maid, and belonged to Timpson, at the coach-office up-street; the locomotive engine that had brought me back, was called severely No. 97, and belonged to S.E.R., and was spitting ashes and hot water over the blighted ground.

The winding River Medway, secluded from the Thames but not too far from the capital, made Chatham an appropriate location for the naval base. It functioned as such from the sixteenth century to 1984 when dockyard and naval barracks both closed. In a naval equivalent to swords being turned into ploughshares, wharves for battleships have been transformed into marinas for pleasure craft. The town has been ravaged by developers and a sad atmosphere prevails with a tang of having seen better and more meaningful times. Much of the Georgian dockyard has survived and is now a museum. So has the elegant Command House, on Riverside Gardens, overlooking the site of the original Tudor dockyard. But other examples of the eighteenth-century architectural heritage have been destroyed, either by enemy action or by insensitive 'improvements'.

Dickens's first home here was in Ordnance Terrace. It was fictionalised as Gordon Place in the story 'Old Lady' in *Sketches by Boz*. In the same book there are other memories of Ordnance Terrace. The story 'Our Parish' has an old lady based on a kindly neighbour, Mrs Newnham. In the same story, the Half Pay Captain was based on another resident of the Terrace. And James Steerforth in *David Copperfield* was possibly based on George Stroughill, another neighbour. The household had a maidservant called Mary Weller, whose surname was probably the inspiration for the name of Dickens's first great comic creation.

Overlooking the railway station, the Terrace still happily survives. In the late 1960s the whole terrace was threatened with demolition, on the pretext that it needed to be restored. It is an elegant late-eighteenth-century group of houses, with a plaque on the house Dickens occupied. The windows of the upper floors command a view of the whole town of Chatham, and of the Medway.

In his 1860 piece 'Dullborough Town', written for *All the Year Round*, he wrote:

I began to look about me; and the first discovery I made, was, that the Station had swallowed up the playing-field

Ordnance Terrace, Chatham

[where as a lad] ... in the hay-making time, [he had] been delivered from the dungeons of Seringapatam, an immense pile (of hollyhock), by my own countrymen, the victorious British (boy next door and his two cousins). And had been recognised with ecstasy by my affianced one (Miss Green), who had come all the way from England (second house in the terrace) to ransome me, and marry me.

Dickens was never nostalgic about a pre-industrial Britain. He welcomed scientific and technological innovations. Any nostalgia he had was for the vision of his childhood; that playing field had stirred his child's imagination and now it 'was gone. The two beautiful hawthorn-trees, the hedge, the turf, and all those buttercups and daisies, had given place to the stoniest of jolting roads: while, beyond the Station, an ugly dark monster of a tunnel kept its jaws open, as if it had swallowed them and were ravenous for more destruction.'

Ordnance Terrace leads to some hilly parkland that looks down on New Road, now the main road from Rochester to Canterbury. This New Road was built at the end of the eighteenth century to bypass the centre of Chatham. The parkland used to be the grounds of Fort Pitt, built while Dickens was a boy in Chatham. The fort was turned into a military hospital and then became a girls' school. The grounds were later transformed into the park. It was at 'sunset, in a lonely field beyond Fort Pitt' that Mr Winkle, in *The Pickwick Papers*, nearly fought his duel with Doctor Slammer of the 97th Regiment.

In 1821 the Dickens family moved to cheaper quarters – to 18 St Mary's Place. The house they lived in was next door to the Providence Baptist Church of the young Reverend William

Giles. Dickens attended a school run by him until June 1823. He was head boy and Giles inspired him. When Dickens's parents left Chatham at the end of 1822, moving to London, Charles stayed on with the Giles family. When he left, Giles gave him a packet of books and later, after the success of *The Pickwick Papers*, Giles sent a snuff box, addressed to *The Inimitable Boz*. Dickens cherished this title for the rest of his life.

At St Mary's Place the Dickens family took in a lodger, Dr Matthew Lamert, who may have been the model for Dr Slammer in *The Pickwick Papers*. Dr Lamert married Mary Allen, the widowed sister of Charles's mother. Lamert's son from his previous marriage took young Charles to the theatre in Rochester. (A few years later he also introduced him to the work of the blacking factory at Hungerford Stairs.) There is today nothing to indicate young Charles Dickens's second Chatham home. The house suffered damage in the Second World War and was later pulled down. Today the Iceland car park occupies the site. The chapel next door became a Salvation Army drill hall and the building lasted until the 1990s. The area, the Brook, now a busy through road, was for many years the town's red light district, the clientele being sailors on leave. As late as the 1940s the navy used to issue leave-bound sailors contraceptives.

The Brook is crossed by the High Street. To the west it is pedestrianised. Most of the buildings are from the post-Dickens nineteenth and twentieth centuries. Many places associated with Dickens's childhood have gone. There was a public house, the Mitre, where the boy Dickens used to sing comic songs. In the nineteenth century it was called The Mitre Inn and Clarence Hotel – for the Duke of Clarence, later King

William IV, stayed here. In a lesser-known Christmas story, 'The Holly Tree Inn', written in 1855, the narrator recalls this inn and how 'I loved the landlord's youngest daughter to distraction – but let that pass. It was in this Inn that I was cried over by my rosy little sister, because I had acquired a black-eye in a fight'. The site of the inn is now occupied by a Primark.

To the east of the Brook is the Gala Bingo Hall, which is on the site of the workhouse. When the Dickens family were at St Mary's Place they recruited a diminutive servant girl from the workhouse who became the model for the Marchioness in *The Old Curiosity Shop*. This was probably the first workhouse that Dickens was aware of – presumably providing material for *Oliver Twist*. Incidentally Mudfog is a name applied both to the location of Oliver's workhouse and also to Chatham in the 'Mudfog Papers', stories he wrote for *Bentley's Miscellany* in 1837. Oliver Twist's Mudfog is north of London, for Oliver walks to London via Barnet. But the other Mudfog is a maritime town:

> Mudfog is a pleasant town – a remarkably pleasant town – situated in a charming hollow by the side of a river, from which river, Mudfog derives an agreeable scent of pitch, tar, coals, and rope yarn, a roving population in oil skin hats, a pretty steady influx of drunken bargemen, and a great many other maritime advantages. There is a good deal of water about Mudfog, and yet it is not exactly the sort of town for a watering place, either.

Nearby is Institute Road, where in the middle of the nineteenth century there was a Mechanics Institute, providing education for the working classes. Dickens was a great supporter of these Institutes and in 1861 helped to raise funds for this one, giving six readings in the Chatham Opera House, on the site of which there is now a shop at 205 High Street.

This part of Chatham lies in the shadow of the Lines, the open country to the east. A twentieth-century war memorial is the hub of a number of footpaths over this public parkland. The site of a large car park beyond the war memorial is where the Pickwickians, with Mr Wardle, witnessed the military review:

> the whole population of Rochester and the adjoining towns rose from their beds at an early hour ... in a state of the utmost bustle and excitement. A grand review was to take place upon the Lines. The manoeuvres of half-a-dozen regiments were to be inspected by the eagle eye of the commander-in-chief; temporary fortifications had been erected, the citadel was to be attacked and taken, and a mine was to be sprung.

It is windy up here, and was so when Mr Pickwick was there. The wind snatched away his hat and the poor man had to chase after it; the hat and Mr Pickwick were rescued by Mr Wardle, and this was the beginning of a beautiful friendship.

When Dickens moved back to Kent, to Gad's Hill Place, he often revisited the sites of his childhood. On one occasion he wandered up to the Lines. 'I took a walk upon these Lines and mused among the fortifications, grassy and innocent enough on the surface at present, but tough subjects at the core.'

To the north is Fort Amherst, built in 1756 to guard the

landward approach to the dockyard. In its vicinity David Copperfield spent a night. He 'crept, at last, upon a sort of grass-grown battery overhanging a lane, where a sentry was walking to and fro. Here I lay down, near a cannon; and, happy in the society of the sentry's footsteps ... slept soundly until morning.'

Beyond is Chatham Dockyard itself. John Dickens used to go regularly to Sheerness to pay the employees of the dockyard there. Sometimes he would sail on a seventeenth-century yacht, taking the young Charles and his older sister, Frances (Fanny) with him.

Many years later Dickens became friends with an aristocratic lady, Mary Boyle, a forgotten novelist and a fellow amateur actor. He met her through her relations, Mr and Mrs Watsons of Rockingham Castle, the model for Chesney Wold in *Bleak House*. Dickens had met the Watsons on one of his European sojourns. At Rockingham he took part with his upper-class friends in amateur dramatics and played Sir Peter Teazle opposite Mary's Lady Teazle. It was an improbable friendship, but they had Sheerness in common. Mary was two years older than Dickens and her father had been commissioner of Sheerness Docks. If they never met when they were children, they at least had North Kent in common.

Around the Medway Towns

The Marshes

> Ours was the marsh country, down by the river, within,
> as the river wound, twenty miles of the sea ... the dark flat
> wilderness beyond the churchyard, intersected with dykes
> and mounds and gates, with scattered cattle feeding on it,
> was the marshes; and ... the low leaden line beyond, was
> the river ...

IN THIS WAY, the scene is set at the opening of *Great Expectations*, the novel published serially from 1860 to 1861 and the first work written after Dickens's return to Kent and his residence at Gad's Hill. Oddly enough he does not name places but much of the novel reflects Dickens's rediscovery of a part of the country he had known as a child forty years earlier – the time of the setting of the novel. Rochester is not mentioned by name but it is clearly the novel's 'market town'.

The marshes – or 'th'meshes' as both Joe and Mrs Gargery call them – are recognisable from Dicken's description: the dykes, the mounds and the gates, the scattered cattle. Some things have changed however; there is now a sea wall along the Thames and the land is no longer subject to flooding at high tide. The castle at Cooling used to be a Thames-side fort when built in the fourteenth century but today the river is two or more miles away. There are no longer prison hulks but there is a sense of brooding menace and desolation about the place. This can best be captured in the winter. It was Christmas Eve when Magwitch surprised Pip in the first chapter of *Great Expectations*.

In January I walked east of Gravesend on the 'Saxon Shore Way'. On the edge of Gravesend is the Ship and Lobster Inn, claiming to be the first and last pub on the River Thames. It may have been The Ship in *Great Expectations*. I left before 8:00 a.m. There was a seasonal mist and I could hear the fog-horns of ships as they made their way up or down the Thames, but I was unable to see them. For the whole day the Essex coast was out of sight. I walked about fifteen miles along by the sea wall and met nobody. It was bitterly cold with occasional flakes of snow. I could not stop for more than ten minutes for fear of being frozen to immobility. I sympathised with Magwitch and Compeyson for the night they spent on these marshes. But people had passed by recently, to judge from the human detritus I came across. One mile from Gravesend I found two or three rusting supermarket trolleys. After that I came upon a recently inflated balloon. And then a football. How had each of these items ended up on this path?

On each side of the Thames are forts, part of the defences of outer London. The first to be seen outside Gravesend is Shornemead Fort, built in the 1790s but redeveloped in the middle of the following century. It is a ruin, neglected and decaying: unwanted. The path curves to the north to a larger fort, Cliffe Fort, built in the 1860s opposite Coalhouse Fort on the Essex coast. The engineer responsible for constructing these forts was General Charles Gordon, later killed in Khartoum. Either of these forts could have served as the Battery in the early chapters of *Great Expectations*. It was a place Joe and Pip escaped for larky chats away from the unlarky chidings of Mrs Joe.

The village of Cliffe is now a mile from the sea, but it was once a port. A cordite factory and cement works have not added to its charms, but it has had its moments of history. It used to be called Bishop's Cliffe and was the location of meetings of Saxon bishops in the province of Canterbury. It has been argued that this was the first parliamentary system in England.

East of Cliffe Fort there is little to distract the eye. But it is probable that there was a hut – a lime kiln – between the village of Cliffe and the river where Orlick lured Pip in his prosperity and nearly killed him. 'The direction that I took, was not that in which my old home lay ...' Chalk was burnt in lime kilns and the ashes were used as fertiliser. Huts dotted the marshes near the chalky hills. 'It was another half-hour before I drew near to the kiln. The lime was burning with a sluggish stifling smell, but the fires were made up and left, and no workmen were visible. Hard by was a small stone-quarry. It lay directly in my way, and had been worked that day, as I saw by the tools and barrows that were lying about.' As usual, Dickens was very specific in his descriptions and directions.

I turned inland at Egypt Bay, which was one of the mooring sites for the prison hulks. These were ships converted in the eighteenth and nineteenth centuries into prisons to hold convicts who had been sentenced to transportation before they were dispatched to the colonies. North America before independence was first used as a destination for transported criminals, then it was mainly Australia. The hulks were also used to hold prisoners of war during the Napoleonic wars – mainly French but also men from other European countries allied to the French. They were moored near the shore and when the tide was out a lucky and resourceful convict might escape to the sand and mud. He need not have had to swim ashore: at high tide this would have been impossible if he had been in irons. In the sands alongside the Medway estuary the bones and skeletons of prisoners have been found, prisoners who had been unsuccessful in their bid for freedom. The practice of using hulks for prisons in and around the Medway estuary lasted until the 1870s.

Life in the hulks was grim. Convicts were detailed to carry out the toughest of manual labour in the dockyards. One prisoner in *Great Expectations* summed it all up: 'A most beastly place. Mudbank, mist, swamp and work; work, swamp, mist and mudbank.' As I passed Egypt Bay, the tide was out and it was possible to visualise the possible escape of a convict and his coming ashore and making his way through the dykes and marshes to some churchyard where the land began to rise.

I wandered south, away from the Thames. Even the footpaths marked on the map were not clear and it was only after several false starts that I reached a house with the splendidly Dickensian name of Swigshole. From there I walked over the wooded Northward Hill and down to the row of houses by Cooling Church. The names of the houses included one called Magwitch and another known as Fezziwig Cottage (after the family in *A Christmas Carol*). The main concern for residents of Cooling today is the possibility of an estuary airport. Many gardens had a poster protesting against the proposal.

In the cemetery around the parish yard are the graves of ten small children under three-foot-long lozenge-shaped tombstones. The children all died in infancy; six are from the Comport family who lived at Cooling Castle, four others are from another branch of the same family. Does the name Comport suggest the name of Compeyson, Magwitch's fellow prisoner and bitter enemy? Inside the church there is a memorial tablet to the Comport family.

It is unquestionably these graves that inspired Dickens in his description of the graves of Pip's parents and five brothers who all died in infancy. Dickens in his Gad's Hill years liked to bring visitors here. Occasionally he would walk from his home to Cooling Church and back in the afternoon, but he had known Cooling from his childhood in Chatham. Once, in the 1860s, he brought Marcus Stone, the young illustrator of *Our Mutual Friend*, to Cooling. 'You see that church?' Dickens said to Stone, 'That is where I saw the pauper's funeral in Oliver Twist'. The churchyard is more celebrated for the infants' graves and this has led people to see Cooling as the unnamed village where Pip and the Gargerys lived. Indeed one of the cottages is called The Forge. It may indeed have been a forge but in *Great Expectations* Gargery's forge is not near the church. There are other points that work against Cooling's claim. When Magwitch turned Pip upside down 'I saw the steeple under my feet'. Cooling Church has a conical addition to the tower. Hardly a steeple, and certainly not visible if you are turned upside down. (Try it, next time you are there.) The only church in the Hoo peninsula with a steeple is Higham Church, two miles down the road from Gad's Hill, one mile beyond Lower Higham. The church in *Great Expectations* is – like Higham but not Cooling Church – cut off from the village: 'our village lay, on the flat inshore among the alder trees and the pollards, a mile or more from the church'. Moreover in the novel there is a 'gate at the side of the churchyard' that leads on to the open marshes. Dickens was not a regular churchgoer when he was at Gad's Hill but went occasionally to Higham Church and cooperated with the vicar in charitable work. He knew the church, and the location of the churchyard where Pip first met Magwitch fits Higham but not Cooling.

Other factors suggest Lower Higham as the Gargerys' village. Their village had a saw-pit, a windmill, a little shop and a public house. In Higham there was a saw-pit close to the disused canal. In the essay 'Tramps', written in 1860 for *All the Year Round* and reprinted in *The Uncommercial Traveller*, Dickens wrote – a mixture of fact and fiction – about one tramp 'lying drunk ... in the wheelwright's saw-pit under the shed where the felled trees are, opposite the sign of the Three Jolly Hedgers'. This essay was written in 1860, when he was also working on *Great Expectations*. Three Jolly Hedgers is suggestive of Three Jolly Bargemen, the tavern in the Gargerys' village. The old inn in the village used to be The Chequers, but is now closed.

The forge that he may have had in mind was possibly the forge at Chalk, three miles from Gad's Hill just outside Gravesend. 'Joe's forge adjoined our house, which was a wooden house, as many of the dwellings in our country were – most of them, at that time.' The forge at Chalk is a clap-board construction, a common feature of the buildings of coastal Kent.

Of course *Great Expectations* is fiction and not reportage.

Dickens, as we have seen, often described a building or location with such precision that we can identify it. But not infrequently he shifted the buildings around to fit the narrative geography of his novels. It seems that he imagined a village with elements drawn from different places. In *Great Expectations* he teases us by not specifying the places. And why not?

Cobham

... this is one of the prettiest and most desirable places of residence I ever met with.

This is Mr Pickwick's opinion of the village of Cobham when he walked out there through the woods from Rochester. After he moved to Gad's Hill Place it became one of Charles Dickens's favourite walks.

Cobham is separated from the spreading urbanisation of the Medway Towns by two or three miles of woodland and parkland.

A delightful walk it was: for it was a pleasant afternoon in June, and their way lay through a deep and shady wood, cooled by the light wind which gently rustled the thick foliage, and enlivened by the songs of the birds that perched upon the boughs. The ivy and the moss crept in thick clusters over the old trees, and the soft green turf overspread the ground like a silken mat.

From outer Strood a footpath passes under the motorway and over the railway and then up into the woods, part of the estate belonging to Cobham Hall, ancestral home of the Darnleys. The woods and grounds were designed by Humphrey Repton. The earls of Darnley lived at Cobham Hall from the eighteenth to the twentieth century. They derived their income from property in Ireland but during the nineteenth and twentieth centuries life did not go their way. During the second half of the twentieth century they sold the Hall, which is now an independent girls' school, and the grounds, which are today in the care of the National Trust.

The sixth earl of Darnley was a friend of Charles Dickens – Dickens's scorn for the aristocracy was ideological rather than personal and did not prevent him from having cordial relations with noble neighbours. He was invited to use the private grounds of the Darnley estate whenever he wished, and to bring along any friends.

At the top of the climb from Strood we find an octagonal mausoleum – a Grade 1 Listed Building – recently restored and originally designed by James Wyatt for the fourth earl. Nearby, behind some iron fencing, is what is known as the Toe Monument. The fifth earl as a young man came here to show friends how to use an axe, and proceeded to chop off one of his own toes. The monument marks the mishap.

When one emerges from the woods Cobham Hall can be seen to the right. It was built primarily in the sixteenth and early seventeenth centuries,

> the quaint and picturesque architecture of Elizabeth's time ... with eighteenth century additions designed by William Chambers and James Wyatt. Long vistas of stately oaks and elm trees appeared on every side; large herds of deer were

cropping the fresh grass; and occasionally a startled hare
scoured along the ground, with the speed of the shadows
thrown by the light clouds which swept across a sunny landscape like a passing breath of summer.

The Hall and the gardens are featured in Dickens's essay,
'Tramps', in which the Hall is seen through the eyes of an itinerant clock-repairer.

The path becomes a lane and reaches the village of Cobham
at a crossroads. Cobham has three thriving public houses. The
furthest from the park is the Leather Bottle. Here Mr Pickwick, Mr Snodgrass and Mr Winkle tracked down the fugitive
Mr Tupman. 'Having been directed to the Leather Bottle, a
clean and commodious village ale-house, the three travellers
entered, and at once inquired for a gentleman of the name of
Tupman.' They were ushered into the parlour, 'a long, low-
roofed room furnished with a large number of high-backed
leather-cushioned chairs, of fantastic shapes, and embellished
with a great variety of old portraits and roughly-coloured
prints of some antiquity.' Mr Pickwick's room was in the front,
overlooking the churchyard. Here he sat up all night reading
an old clergyman's manuscript.

The inn is still commodious and a warm and friendly place
serving good food. The pictures and prints are worth a careful
study, for this is a Dickensian museum. Many framed prints
are of characters in the novels – Micawber, Mrs Gamp, Peck-
sniff – by various artists. Luke Fildes did the illustrations
for *The Mystery of Edwin Drood* and one print is his moving
drawing of Dickens's study at Gad's Hill after his death – *The
Empty Chair*. (Moving but slightly misleading. Dickens died

in the summer and his last writing was completed, not in the study at Gad's Hill Place, but in the chalet over the road.) There are pictures presented to the inn by Dickens's publishers, Chapman and Hall, and by J. M. Dent, who published the Everyman edition of his works in the twentieth century. One frame has picture postcards of a dozen characters; another is of cigarette cards. As well as many portraits of Dickens, there is also a programme of the Pickwick Bicycle Club, dated 1888. There are no fewer than three copies of a drawing of Mr Jingle by J. Robertson Frith.

Dickens probably came here during his honeymoon at Chalk in April 1836 – he was writing *The Pickwick Papers* at the time. Four years later he returned, bringing his friends; his biographer, John Forster, and the artist Daniel Maclise.

There are also personal relics. His favourite chair is in one room. In another, behind a glass case, is 'the immense leather bag' that accompanied him on his reading tours. Framed nearby is a poster for one of his last readings in 1870 at St James's Hall, Piccadilly. Tickets in the stalls were seven shillings and five shillings, in the balcony three shillings. This was above an admission charge of one shilling. Tickets were available through Keith Prowse and Messrs Chappell, the company that organised the reading tours; both companies a century and a half later are still selling tickets for artistic events.

The most personal, and the most recent exhibit is an authenticated lock of Dickens's hair, barely visible in a glass case. This was the prize in the Dickens fellowship raffle held in early 2013 to raise money for the restoration of the chalet at Eastgate House, Rochester. The winner was a regular at the Leather Bottle and presented the lock, valued at £500, to the inn.

Outside the inn is a stone with cryptic letters:

BILST
UM
PSHI
S.M.
ARK

This reminds us of the episode in *The Pickwick Papers* when Mr Pickwick and his friends puzzled over some identical lettering: 'This is some very old inscription,' said Mr Pickwick, 'existing perhaps long before the ancient alms-houses in this place. It must not be lost.'

The Pickwickians were upstaged in their hypotheses by 'the presumptuous and ill-conditioned Blotton', who,

> with a mean desire to tarnish the lustre of the immortal name of Pickwick, actually undertook a journey to Cobham in person, and on his return, sarcastically observed in an oration at the club, that he had seen the man from whom the stone was purchased; that the man presumed the stone to be ancient, but solemnly denied the antiquity of the inscription – inasmuch as he represented it to have been rudely carved by himself in an idle mood, and to display letters intended to bear neither more nor less than the simple construction of – 'BILL STUMPS, HIS MARK.'

Dickens is mocking the scholarly pretensions of his own creation, but also laughing at the new wave of amateur archaeologists who were recording inscriptions indiscriminately. For example, a few miles away the prehistoric cromlech, Kit's Coty House, between Aylesford and Blue Bell Hill, also had graffiti that had sparked scholarly analysis. Dickens's satirical take on this is an extraordinary piece of confident cheek on the part of a young man of twenty-four.

The 'ancient alms-houses' are behind the Church of St Mary Magdalene (which has some of the finest brass effigies in the country), across the road from the Leather Bottle. Worth a detour, they are called Cobham College and date from the fourteenth century. The architect was probably Henry Yevele, responsible for parts of Westminster Abbey. Originally founded for five priests, the college passed to the family of Lord Cobham after the Reformation and is now, with its modern extension of six flats added in 2012, fulfilling its medieval function as sheltered accommodation for senior citizens.

South of Rochester

I have discovered that the seven miles between Maidstone and Rochester is one of the most beautiful roads in England.

Actually, the distance between the two towns is, according to the milestones, eight miles. Today vehicles are persuaded to take the north–south road further to the east. The main road in Dickens's time was the one that now leaves Rochester High Street just outside the Roman and medieval walls and passes between the Vines and Restoration House before steadily climbing up past the nineteenth-century buildings of Watts's Almshouses, and then, after a mile or so, Rochester Airport. Two motorways cross the road in the course of the eight miles, an erosion of what was once pretty wooded Downland countryside. A ganglion of dual carriageways, slip roads and roundabouts impede the walker in search of the beauties as seen by Dickens. Blue Bell Hill, where Dickens was fond of taking guests, especially American friends, was once as attractive as its name. 'We often take our lunch on a hillside there in the summer, and then I lie down on the grass – a splendid example of laziness.' The woods are tucked away to the west of the main road but now one cannot escape from the drone of the motorway traffic. Blue Bell Hill is today a soulless commuter village.

One of the sites to which Dickens took his guests was Kits Coty, a megalithic burial chamber. For those unfamiliar with the area, this is today hard to find. In the 1840s he wrote to Forster from Broadstairs, proposing a 'walk from Maidstone to Rochester and a visit to the Druidical altar on the wayside [which] are charming.' To the west is the village of Aylesford, with a fourteenth-century ragstone bridge over the Medway. It was formerly a most attractive village, but its charms have been drained away by the inexorable demands of the car and the pressing need to get somewhere else as fast as possible.

In Aylesford churchyard is the tomb of William Spong of Cob Tree. Spong is seen as the probable model for the affable Mr Wardle of Dingley Dell in *The Pickwick Papers*. The chapters on the first visit to Dingley Dell were written about the time Dickens was on his honeymoon at Chalk. It is likely that Dickens met Spong and came to Cob Tree then, and this may have been the prototype of Manor Farm, Dingley Dell. Many of the places in *The Pickwick Papers* are identifiable and without disguise, but it may be that he wanted to spare Spong any embarrassment, or uninvited visitors. There is no lake where Mr Pickwick and friends would have skated on their second visit, but

there is a Manor Farm with a lake at Frindsbury on the northern
outskirts of Strood. It may be that Dickens again shifted that
geographical feature to a site that better suited his story.

> 'Pleasant, pleasant country,' sighed the enthusiastic gentle-
> man, as he opened his lattice window. 'Who could live to
> gaze from day to day on bricks and slates, who had once felt
> the influence of a scene like this? Who could continue to
> exist, where there are no cows but the cows on the chimney
> pots; nothing redolent of Pan but pan-tiles; no stone but
> stone crop?'

Cobtree Manor Park is now wooded parkland, a sylvan oasis
and retreat from the surrounding motorised environment. It
used to be the site of Maidstone Zoo, and was presented to the
people of Maidstone by Sir Garrard Tyrwhitt-Drake in 1951.

Maidstone itself, with the county headquarters and local
gaol, has lost the quiet charm of earlier decades. It was probably Muggleton in *The Pickwick Papers*: 'a corporate town,
with a mayor, burgesses, and freemen ... an open square for
the market-place, and in the centre a large inn.' There have
been claims for West Malling nearby to have been Muggleton,
but the incorporation seems to tip the matter in Maidstone's
favour. It would have been strange if Dickens, even in his
fiction, overlooked the county town with which he was familiar, if not intimate. In a story told at Dingley Dell, 'The Convict's Return', Dickens has a swipe at those who campaigned
for the abolition of slavery abroad and were, at the same time
– like William Wilberforce – complaisant about the state of
factory workers in the newly industrialised north of England:

Muggleton is an ancient and loyal borough, mingling a zealous advocacy of Christian principles with a devoted attachment to commercial rights; in demonstration whereof, the mayor, corporation, and other inhabitants, have presented at divers times, no fewer than one thousand four hundred and twenty petitions against the continuance of negro slavery abroad, and an equal number against any interference with the factory system at home.

Towards Canterbury

Dickens was less familiar with the countryside between the Medway towns and Canterbury. He travelled along them when he was resident at Gad's Hill Place. But the best description of the road is in *David Copperfield* when David walks to Dover to find his aunt. Having been fleeced at Chatham, footsore and weary, he sets off on Watling Street and limps seven miles before resting by a stream, sleeping under a haystack. He is in hop-country. Along the way he was intimidated by tramps. 'Some of them were ferocious-looking ruffians, who stared at me as I went by; and stopped, perhaps, and called after me to come back, and speak to them; and when I took to my heels, stoned me.'

After having a handkerchief stolen by one tramp who then brutally mistreated his partner, he was so frightened that, whenever 'I saw any of these people coming, I turned back until I could find a hiding-place, where I remained until they had gone out of sight; which happened so often, that I was very seriously delayed.' When Dickens wrote his article on tramps for *The Uncommercial Traveller*, ten years after writing *David*

Copperfield, the alarm of his fictional creation was replaced by humane curiosity about the wayfarers and vagabonds that wandered the Kentish roads in search of a livelihood. They were among those who were at the margins of society, people who stirred his compassionate feelings. He observed the seasonal migration of hoppers, when 'the whole country-side for miles and miles will swarm with hopping tramps. They come in families, men, women, and children, every family provided with a bundle of bedding, an iron pot, a number of babies, and too often with some poor sick creature quite unfit for the rough life, for whom they suppose the smell of the fresh hop to be a sovereign remedy.'

East Kent

Broadstairs

This is a little fishing-place; intensely quiet; built on a cliff, whereon, in the centre of a tiny semicircular bay, our house stands, the sea rolling and dashing under the windows ... Under the cliff are rare good sands, where all the children assemble every morning and throw up impossible fortifications, which the sea throws down again at high-water. Old gentlemen and ancient ladies flirt after their own manner in two reading-rooms and on a great many scattered seats in the open air. Other old gentlemen look all day through telescopes and never see anything. In a bay-window in a one-pair sits, from nine o'clock to one, a gentleman with rather long hair and no neckcloth, who writes and grins as if he thought he were very funny indeed. His name is Boz. At one he disappears, and presently emerges from a bathing-machine, and may be seen – a kind of salmon-coloured porpoise – splashing about in the ocean. After that he may be seen in another bay-window on the ground-floor eating a strong lunch; after that walking a dozen miles or so, or lying on his back in the sand reading a book. Nobody bothers him unless they know he is disposed to be talked to, and I am told he is very comfortable indeed. He's as brown as a berry, and they *do* say is a small fortune to the innkeeper, who sells beer and cold punch.

DICKENS REGULARLY SANG the praises of the small town of Broadstairs, tucked away in a bay between its larger Thanet sisters, Margate and Ramsgate. The area of Thanet, on the north-east coast of Kent, has always had a distinctive personality. The three towns have today merged into one conurbation. Each town centre clings around a pier and an old harbour. Each has a surviving Regency terrace or two. Then the townscape drifts into suburbia and commercial zones, the gaps between buildings being filled up with ... cabbage fields.

Broadstairs was emerging as a fashionable resort for sea bathing in the 1830s, 'for families', as a contemporary guidebook wrote, 'who prefer quiet and retirement to the more noisy pleasures of Margate and Ramsgate'.

Ramsgate also expanded during the years after the French Wars (as they were called at the time). Terraced houses and smart hotels overlooked the harbour. Ramsgate was the destination of the newly rich Tuggs family in *Sketches by Boz*, in preference to Gravesend ('low') and Margate ('commercial'). The family took an outing on donkey-back to Pegwell Bay to the south. Today Ramsgate is the largest of the three Thanet towns.

Margate had been a pioneer resort in the late eighteenth century. Benjamin Beale is credited as the first pioneer of the bathing machine, and a fashionable town grew up on the hill above the old fishing village. With one or two terraces, a smart square, Cecil Square, and a Theatre Royal dating from 1787 and still functioning – the visitor can still identify traces of a smarter Margate. The town was the birthplace of the painter J. M. W. Turner in 1775 and of the artist Tracey Emin nearly 200 years later.

Dickens first came to Broadstairs in 1837, bringing his wife and infant son, Charley, and staying at 12 High Street, a modest cottage, long gone and replaced by a shop (number 31) over which, in March, there was still a Christmas decoration. A plaque records Dickens's residence here. It was not over-looking the sea; although he had just become famous with the publication of *The Pickwick Papers*, he was not yet financially secure enough or confident enough to rent accommodation nearer the sea. 'I have seen ladies and gentlemen walking upon the earth in slippers of buff,' he observed on that visit, 'pickling themselves in the sea in complete suits of the same ... I have found that our next door neighbour has a wife and something else under the same roof with the rest of the furniture – the wife deaf and blind, and the something else given to drinking.' His rooms looked out on to urban, not maritime views. 'You would hardly guess which is the main street of our watering-place, but you may know it by its being always stopped up with donkey-chaises. Whenever you come here, and see harnessed donkeys eating clover out of barrows drawn completely across a narrow thoroughfare, you may be quite sure you are in our High Street.'

Dickens made Broadstairs his home for a few months every summer or autumn for the next ten years. It was already a favourite resort of Dickens's actor friend, William Macready. In 1839 Dickens stayed at 40 Albion Street, nearer the sea and now part of the Albion Hotel. It was not too comfortable. There was a bower 'which is shaded for you in the one-pair front, where no chair or table has four legs of the same length, and where no drawers will open till you have pulled the pegs off, and then they keep open and won't shut again'. The proximity to the sea made him more sensitive to its moods. Last night, he wrote to John Forster, 'there was such a sea! I staggered down to the pier and, creeping under the lee of a large boat which was high and dry, watched it breaking for nearly an hour. Of course I came back wet through.' *Nicholas Nickleby* was completed during this summer. He dedicated the book to Macready.

The following year he took Lawn House, in a small square off Harbour Street. This is now Archway House. At the time, 1840, he was writing *The Old Curiosity Shop* and *Barnaby Rudge*.

Dickens's routines in writing were becoming fixed. He rose early and spent four hours writing. In the afternoon he went for energetic walks but often with friends and family whom he invited to Broadstairs – they had to look after themselves during the morning. After his walking he was ready to be social. He would walk with his family to the beach and to the pier. 'We have a pier – a queer old wooden pier, fortunately – without the slightest pretensions to architecture, and very picturesque in consequence. Boats are hauled upon it, ropes are coiled all over it; lobster-pots, nets, masts, oars, spars, sails, ballast, and rickety capstans, make a perfect labyrinth of it.' It was Broadstairs in 1840 that was the scene of his first serious flirtation. He met a young lady, Eleanor Picken (who at twenty, was eight years his junior) at a party where there was some dancing. Eleanor later became a writer herself and, after Dickens's death, recorded her encounter, which must have been initially thrilling, but subsequently alarming. Inviting her to dance, he adopted a mock-archaic language: 'Wilt tread a measure with me, sweet lady? Fain would I thread the mazes of the saraband with thee.'

To which she replied, 'Aye, fair Sir, that I will right gladly. In good sooth, I'll never say Nay.'

They met in the daytime, in a group walking by the sea. On the jetty they danced a quadrille. Dickens's wife, as well as his younger brother, Frederick, was with them. He whistled a tune and Charles accompanied him on a pocket comb. Suddenly Dickens swept Eleanor off to the end of the jetty, grabbed her, and threatened to cast himself and her into the sea. She was suddenly scared. Her silk dress was soaked up to her knees and she screamed: 'Mrs Dickens, help me! Make Mr Dickens let me go.'

Whereupon Catherine Dickens chided her husband: 'Charles, how can you be so silly? You will both be carried off by the tide, and you'll spoil the poor girl's dress.'

'Talk not to me of dress!' Eleanor reported Dickens as saying, 'When the pall of Night is enshrouding me in Cimmerian darkness, when we already stand on the brink of the great mystery, shall our thoughts be of fleshly vanities?'

This scene aside, Dickens was able to relax in Broadstairs in a way that seemed to be impossible in London: 'I am in an exquisitely lazy state, bathing, walking, reading, lying in the sun, doing everything but working'.

The walking would be intensive. He would be observing people and buildings, everything. Sometimes his wanderings took him inland, away from the sea. The old village of Broadstairs was a mile from the bay, and was built around the

Church of St Peter's, which he saw as 'a hideous temple of flint, like a petrified haystack.' In 1845 he stayed at the Albion Hotel. He wrote to a friend, telling him he had 'walked 20 miles a day since I came down, and went to a circus at Ramsgate on Saturday night'.

The sea was often rough. It had inspired Turner, and also thrilled Dickens. Until the coming of the railway in 1846, the main way of reaching the Thanet towns from London was by boat. September 1842 was particularly stormy: 'the sea is running so high that we have no choice but to return by land. No steamer can come out of Ramsgate, and the Margate boat lay out all night on Wednesday with all her passengers on board ... We cannot open a window, or a door; legs are no use on the terrace; and the Margate boats can only take people aboard at Herne Bay'. Dickens, nonetheless, was fascinated by storms. The impressions of the storms were stored in his mind and were brought out in his description in *David Copperfield* of the storm that destroyed James Steerforth's boat. That took place at Yarmouth, but it was a Thanet storm Dickens had observed and was describing. The death of Steerforth, written at Broadstairs, was one of his favourite passages in his readings.

In the last two years of the 1840s Dickens took a flat at Chandos Place, south of the pier near what is today called Viking Bay. The flat looked 'out upon a dark, grey sea, with a keen north-east wind blowing it in shore'. The railway brought more trippers. Dickens's portrait by Maclise was reproduced in his books, and Dickens was becoming a recognisable celebrity – indeed, part of the attraction of the town.

At home, Dickens was able to impose silence on his household so he could work during the mornings, but he could not control distractions outside the home. In 1848 he was complaining about the noise:

> Vagrant music is getting to that height here, and is so impossible to be escaped from, that I fear that Broadstairs and I must part company in time to come. Unless it pours with rain I cannot write half-an-hour without the most excruciating organs, fiddles, bells, or glee-singers. There is a violin of the most torturing kind under the window now (time, ten in the morning) and an Italian box of music on the steps – both in full blast.

The following year he went to Bonchurch on the Isle of Wight in pursuit of tranquillity. Perhaps there was too much quiet, for he returned to Broadstairs later in the year, putting up at the Albion Hotel. 'It is a rough little place, but a very pleasant one', he wrote to a friend.

He was drawn to the elemental maritime character of Broadstairs. He wrote to friends constantly, wanting them to share the place with him, if not in person, at least through the allure of his descriptions. 'The ocean lies winking in the sunlight like a drowsy lion,' he wrote about the town at low tide. Its 'glassy waters scarcely curve upon the shore; the fishing-boats in the tiny harbour are all stranded in the mud ... Rusty cables and chains, ropes and rings, undermost parts of posts and piles, and confused timber defences against the waves, lie strewn about in a brown litter of tangled seaweed and fallen cliff ... The time when this pretty little semicircular sweep of houses, tapering off at the end of the wooden pier into a point in the sea, was a gay place.' And then, by contrast, at high tide: 'The

Fort House, Broadstairs

tide has risen; the boats are dancing on the bubbling water; the colliers are afloat again; the white-bordered waves rush in ... The radiant sails are gliding past the shore and shining on the far horizon; all the sea is sparkling, heaving, swelling up with life and beauty this bright morning.'

He had always wanted to rent Fort House for the season. This was the house on the Kingsgate road on the hill overlooking the harbour, pier and bay, and insulated from the din of trippers. It had been built in a mock Gothic style in 1801 for the commander of a fort that was next to the house. In the middle of the nineteenth century it was separated from the sea by a cornfield. The house became available in 1850 and he rented it that year and in the following year. ('It is more delightful here than I can express,' he wrote in 1851. 'Corn growing, larks singing, garden full of flowers, fresh air on the sea. – O it is wonderful!') The building was popularly known as Bleak House before Dickens came to Broadstairs, although at that time it was formally listed as Fort House. After Dickens's time it was renamed Bleak House, even though not a word of that novel was written there and this Broadstairs house does not actually feature in the novel – Esther Summerson's visit to Deal, on the coast towards Dover, was the nearest reference to the town. The Bleak House of the novel was clearly located in Hertfordshire near St Albans, although it is possible that some of the features of Fort House were reproduced in the fictional house – as Dickens did with other places. Some of the rooms are named after novels, but the room most redolent of Dickens is the study. Dickens's desk is in a niche overlooking the sea, where he could have drawn inspiration from the view – still or stormy, always studded with boats. The study's walls display photographs of the author – and one of Nelly Ternan – as well as prints of some of his fictional creations. Personal mementos include a pen-knife and a garden chair brought here from Gad's Hill Place. On the wall outside is a plaque, recording Dickens's connection. The relief portrait of him depicts the older bearded Dickens – an odd touch for it was only after he was a regular visitor to Broadstairs that he grew the beard.

Another transfer of a building from one place to an alternative fictional location was Dickens's use of Betsey Trotwood's home. In *David Copperfield* her house is on a cliff near Dover. Much of that novel was written in Broadstairs. Over the years – especially when he had stayed at the Albion Hotel, he had got to know a forceful lady, Mary Pearson Strong, who lived in a house in Nuckle's Place, south of the hotel. Her house is now the Dickens Museum. In the 1840s her property extended to the cliff edge. Today Victoria Parade separates the garden of the cottage from the cliff. She was the model for Betsey Trotwood, both in her robust and kindly nature, and in her ferocity towards people who brought donkeys near the house. ('Janet ... Donkeys!') Dickens's son, Charley, remembered her as a charming old lady who often fed him tea and cakes. The house was the model for Betsey's cottage which was transferred to the cliffs above Dover: 'a very neat little cottage with cheerful bow windows; in front of it, a small square gravelled court or garden, full of flowers carefully tended, and smelling deliciously'.

Her parlour, the first room on the right as you enter, was described as Betsey's parlour. The house became known as Dickens's House at the end of the nineteenth century and became a museum in the early 1970s. There are letters of Dickens's on display, as well as furniture that belonged to him. Framed collections of cigarette cards – of places associated with Dickens and of the characters in his novels – are reminders of a cultural world of fifty or sixty years ago when smoking promoted popular education. Posters, older pictures of the town, and some of the old serial numbers of the novels fill the museum, managed with enthusiasm and encyclopaedic expertise by Eddie and Lee Ault.

Dickens did not always bring his wife to Broadstairs. In 1850,

Catherine Dickens gave birth in London to their third daughter, Dora, named after David Copperfield's first wife – who had herself been based on Dickens's first love, Maria Beadnell. Dickens was in London for the birth but came back to Broadstairs alone by an afternoon train. He explained to his wife, 'I still have Dora to kill – I mean the Copperfield Dora'. Not a very gallant remark to his wife who suffered discomfort from her ten pregnancies. It appeared utterly callous in the light of the fact that this daughter Dora died two years later. Was this the beginning of the end for Dickens's marriage? He seemed to resent the fact that his wife was so frequently pregnant – as if he had had nothing to do with it. He had wanted her to have little girls – replacements for her sister, upon whom Charles Dickens had doted until she died in his arms at the age of seventeen. But his wife produced seven sons, and only two daughters who survived infancy.

At one point when he was writing *David Copperfield*, Dickens ran out of paper. There was a stationery shop in the High Street near the junction with Albion Road. It also sold magazines, and he went to buy some more paper. A lady was ahead of him and asking for the latest serial number of *David Copperfield*. She was handed a number.

'I've already got that,' she said. 'I want the next number.'

'That won't be out until the end of the month', she was told.

'Listening to this, unrecognised,' Dickens recalled, 'knowing the purpose for which I was there, and remembering that not one word of the number she was asking for was yet written, for the first and only time in my life, I felt – frightened.'

1851 was the last year he spent time in Broadstairs. That year he wrote an affectionate account of the place in *Household*

Words – 'Our Watering Place'. It was a valedictory essay, for he only came back once after that – in 1859, prior to a reading tour.

Although Broadstairs became identified with Dickens, it was only in the twentieth century that Dickens tourism took off. The 1892 *Murray's Guide to Kent* makes no reference to Dickens's sojourns in the town. But since then there have been several plaques as well as a Barnaby Rudge pub, a Trotwood Place, a Nickleby Take Away Café (Thai cuisine) and Bumble's Antiques, as well as the Dickens Museum and Bleak House.

Broadstairs has retained the character of the smallest and most elegant of the three major Thanet towns. When the nouveau-riche Tuggs family in *Sketches by Boz* are wondering where to spend a season, Gravesend, as we have seen, is rejected as 'low'. Margate was worse – 'nobody there but tradespeople'. Broadstairs does not get a mention, but they finally opt for neighbouring Ramsgate, which they find sufficiently genteel.

Margate

Margate has always had a rough reputation. Dickens did visit the town – he went to the theatre there several times in the 1840s. The theatre still functions and has recently been refurbished. But there are hints that he was also familiar with the red light district of the town, for in 1841 he wrote to Daniel Maclise suggesting that he might like to visit the prostitutes of Margate – 'I know where they live', he told the artist archly. Dickens was always interested in the people at the margins of society and did heroic social work with Baroness Burdett-Coutts in providing a refuge in Shepherd's Bush for vulnerable and abused women. He was still a happily married man in 1841, but it is likely that he had walked around the seedier parts of the town. After the collapse of his marriage it is possible that he did find outlets for his sexual energies. In the summer of 1859 he wrote to his doctor about a 'small malady' arising from his 'bachelor state'; this is interpreted as a reference to some venereal disease he had contracted. It is reasonable to infer that Nelly Ternan did not become Dickens's mistress until some years after he first became infatuated with her.

Nelly was a remarkable and resourceful lady. Over the twelve years of her relationship with Dickens she had to be, in the word used in Claire Tomalin's biography of her, *invisible*. After Dickens died she spent time with family in Europe and then returned to England and stayed with her sister in Oxford. There she met a young Oxford graduate in holy orders, George Wharton Robinson, twelve years younger than her. Nelly took fourteen years off her age, making her apparently a suitable two years younger than the unsuspecting George. They fell in love and married, and Nelly had two children. Husband and children knew there was some family friendship with Dickens but had no idea of her actual past. After all she had, they believed, been only seventeen when Dickens had died.

In 1877 the Reverend and Mrs Robinson came to Margate, where he became head of Margate High School. The school occupied a spacious site near the centre of the town and close to the sea; the site is now occupied by a supermarket, though the name College Walk is an echo of the former establishment. Their house was on Hawley Street. Nelly was able to play the part of headmaster's wife and was involved in local amateur dramatics. One of the roles she took was that of Mrs Jarley, the owner of the waxworks in *The Old Curiosity Shop*.

She may have kept her liaison with Dickens from her immediate family, but she did find a confidant in the vicar of St John's Church, Margate, the Reverend (later Canon) William Benham. He later disclosed her story to Thomas Wright who, in 1935, after Nelly, the Canon and all Charles Dickens's children were dead, made it public in a biography of Dickens. Since then more and more details of the extraordinary story of Dickens's relations with Nelly have seeped out.

Deal

Deal, equidistant between Ramsgate and Dover, has over the years been a garrison and naval town. Its castle was part of the nation's defences built by King Henry VIII. It was also home to a station of the Life Boat service, of which Dickens was a great admirer.

> These are among the bravest and most skilful mariners that exist. Let a gale rise and swell into a storm, and let a sea run that might appall the stoutest heart that ever beat; let the light ships on the sands throw up a rocket in the darkness of the night; or let them hear through the angry roar the signal guns of a ship in distress, and these men spring up with activity so dauntless, so valiant and heroic, that the world cannot surpass it.

Esther Summerson in *Bleak House* came to Deal where the feckless Richard Carstone was stationed. She came into the narrow streets of Deal and very gloomy they were, upon a raw misty morning. The long flat beach with its little irregular houses, wooden and brick, and its litter of capstans, and great boats and sheds, and bare upright poles with tackle and blocks, and loose gravely waste places overgrown with grass and weeds, were as dull an appearance as any place I ever saw ... But when we got into a warm room in an excellent hotel ... Deal began to look more cheerful.

Dickens walked to Deal from Dover in 1858, a visit that became an essay published the following year in *Household Words*: 'A walk of ten miles brought me to a seaside town without a cliff, which, like the town I had come from, was out of the season too. Half of the houses were shut up; half of the other half were to let; the town might have done as much business as it was doing then, if it had been at the bottom of the sea.' Dickens was only a little more positive about the place than William Cobbett, who came here in 1823 and found it 'a most villainous place. It is full of filthy-looking people.'

Today Deal is a quiet town, easily overshadowed by its larger neighbours, but still with its pier, museums and castle.

Dover

After noise chased Dickens away from Broadstairs, he tried Dover, a town that had several functions. It was a fishing town, one of the main ports for travel to the European continent – the English Channel is at its narrowest here – and, in parallel with many other seaside towns in the south-east, a smart and fashionable resort. It has also been a major base for the defence of England – with a castle, fortifications and a military history that goes back two millennia.

Today the social geography of the town reflects these functions. Townwall Street brings traffic rushing to join the embarkation queues, slicing the smarter early nineteenth century town from the older town nestling under the cliffs.

Dover had already appeared in *David Copperfield*. Betsey Trotwood lived at Dover, and, having walked from London, the weary David sat down, 'on the step of an empty shop at a street corner, near the market place'. A coffee house, Dickens Corner, once marked the place where David collapsed before a kindly driver told him where his aunt lived. A plaque records the fictional event. Betsey Trotwood's cottage was on the cliffs, but the house he described was the house in Broadstairs.

The little narrow, crooked town of Dover hid itself away from the beach, and ran its head into the chalk cliffs, like a marine ostrich. The beach was a desert of heaps of sea and stones tumbling wildly about, and the sea did what it liked, and what it liked was destruction. It thundered at the town, and thundered at the cliffs, and brought the coast down, madly. The air among the houses was of so strong a piscatory flavour that one might have supposed sick fish went up to be dipped in it, as sick people went down to be dipped in the sea. A little fishing was done in the port, and a quantity of strolling about at night, and looking seaward ... Small tradesmen, who did no business whatever, sometimes unaccountably realised large fortunes, and it was remarkable that nobody in the neighbourhood could endure a lamplighter.

Dickens brought his family here in 1852. 'It is not quite a place to my taste, being too bandy (I mean musical; no reference to its legs), and infinitely too genteel. But the sea is very fine, and the walks are quite remarkable.' They stayed at 10 Camden Crescent for three months, during which Dickens wrote parts of *Bleak House*. Number 10 has disappeared but outside number 17 a plaque records Dickens's one-time residence nearby.

To the west is Harbour House. This used to be the grand hotel of the town, the Lord Warden, built in the early 1850s. Dickens was an early guest, staying there in 1855 and again in 1861. On the former occasion he visited the theatre in Snargate Street, built at the end of the eighteenth century and long since destroyed. It was 'a miserable spectacle – the pit is boarded over, and it is a drinking and smoking place'. On the latter visit he gave some readings, and thought that the audience had 'the greatest sense of humour'.

Folkestone

... it was a little fishing town, and they do say that the time was when it was a little smuggling town ... The old little fishing and smuggling town remains ... There are breakneck flights of ragged steps, connecting the principal streets by backways, which will cripple the visitor in half an hour ... Our situation is delightful, our air delicious, and our breezy hills and downs, carpeted with wild thyme, and decorated with millions of wild flowers, are, in the faith of the pedestrian, perfect.

Royal Pavilion Hotel, Folkestone

In March 2013 *The Times* wrote that Folkestone was the fifth coolest place in Britain. For a generation it was yet another declining seaside resort but the former owner of Saga, Roger de Haan, has invested money with the expectation of a regeneration. It has a promising future.

Dickens made several visits to the town. It was quieter than Dover, and he came here in 1855, when he was seeking somewhere to replace Broadstairs. He stayed with his family at 3 Albion Villas – 'a very pleasant little house, overlooking the sea' – just before the publication of *Little Dorrit*. Today the house has a plaque and still looks down on the cliffs and beach. The great hotel of the town was the Royal Pavilion Hotel, built in 1843. It has been replaced by the Grand Burstin Hotel, which could be anywhere in the world. Dickens stayed at its predecessor and wrote about Folkestone in an article, 'Out of Town', written in 1855 for *Household Words*. In the piece Folkestone is Pavilionstone, named after the hotel. The hotel was built about 100 yards from the railway terminus, Folkestone Harbour Station. The new hotel was a great improvement on existing conditions for travellers; previously they were accommodated in 'a strange building which had just left off being a barn without having quite begun to be a house.' The hotel, by contrast, provided every comfort:

> you walk into that establishment as if it were your club; and find ready for you, your news-room, dining-room, smoking-room, billiard-room, music-room, public breakfast, public dinner, twice a day (one plain, one gorgeous), hot baths and cold baths. If you want to be bored, there are plenty of bores always ready for you.

The Channel Tunnel has taken custom away from Folkestone as a port. Folkestone Harbour Station, neglected and falling into ruin, was formally closed in 2014, along with the line. The new hotel incorporates some of the old Royal Pavilion. Some furniture survives and the kitchens in the basement are original. The hotel is a refuge for older people of Folkestone, with bars, restaurants, gaming saloons and non-stop television in one of the lounges.

Canterbury

> The sunny street of Canterbury, dozing, as it were, in the
> hot light ... its old houses and gateways, and the stately gray
> cathedral, with the rooks sailing round the towers.

Canterbury features centrally in only one of Dickens's novels –
David Copperfield. Dickens never lived in or close to it, so the
descriptions lack the intimacy of those of the Medway towns
or Thanet. He visited and got to know the city well, however,
and was fond in his last years of taking friends here. He was
not always a fan of medieval architecture but appreciated the
picturesque, and historical associations.

> The venerable cathedral towers and the old jackdaws and
> rooks, whose airy voices made them more retired than
> perfect silence would have done; the battered gateways,
> once stuck full with statues, long thrown down, and crum-
> bled away, like the reverential pilgrims who had gazed upon
> them; the still nooks, where the ivied growth of centuries
> crept over gabled ends and ruined walls; the ancient houses;
> the pastoral landscape of field, orchard, and garden – eve-
> rywhere, on everything, I felt the same serener air, the same
> calm, thoughtful, softening spirit.

Dickens also used to observe the rooks whirling over Rochester cathedral. There they were compared with the monks of
the past.

When David Copperfield bade farewell to Canterbury he
'sauntered through the dear and tranquil streets, and again
mingled with the shadows of the venerable gateways and

churches. The rooks were sailing about the cathedral towers; and the towers themselves, overlooking many a long unaltered mile of the rich country and its pleasant streams, were cutting the bright morning air, as if there were no such thing as change on earth.'

In Dickens's *A Child's History of England*, written just after he had completed *David Copperfield*, there is a sense of place in his account of the murder of Becket in 1170. He wrote how 'there was a near way between [Becket's] Palace and the Cathedral, by some beautiful old cloisters which you may yet see'. He described the angular nature of the interior, where 'there were so many hiding-places in the crypt below and in the narrow passages above, that Thomas à Becket might even at that pass have saved himself'.

The visitor to the cathedral today has to pay £17 for the privilege. Entry to the cathedral at Rochester – and also Durham – is free; visitors are instead invited to make a donation. It is unfortunate that the less well-off and those on benefits are not encouraged to go inside Canterbury Cathedral. My first visit was by myself when I was twelve years old. In my twenties I was passing through Canterbury and took a few minutes off to drop into the place, went into the Romanesque crypt and by chance heard an organ playing a Bach passacaglia and fugue: an intensely memorable experience. High entry charges deter the curious cash-strapped young from these intense aesthetic encounters. The ticket barrier has been set up at Christchurch Gate, next door to the Starbucks café. Today I do not go into the cathedral; I do however go into Rochester Cathedral and voluntarily pay the amount Canterbury would have charged me.

Much of the traffic has been banished from central Canterbury. This has made it a safe place to wander round. It was not always so. Betsey Trotwood used to come from Dover to the city in her pony and trap. As David Copperfield recorded,

My aunt had a great opportunity of insinuating the gray pony among carts, baskets, vegetables, and hucksters' goods. The hair-breadth turns and twists we made drew down upon us a variety of speeches from the people standing about, which were not always complimentary; but my aunt drove on with perfect indifference, and I dare say would have taken her own way with as much coolness through an enemy's country.

Betsey Trotwood came to Canterbury to see David, whom she had placed in Dr Strong's school. This is possibly based on King's School, which was a 'grave building in a courtyard, with a learned air about it that seemed well suited to the stray rooks and jackdaws who came down from the cathedral towers to walk with a clerkly bearing on the grass plot.' The main part of King's School is to the east of the city walls. Between here and the city walls is Lady Wootton's Green. Here, at number 1, was the home of the fictional school's lexicographer headmaster, Dr Strong. In the secluded garden 'peaches were ripening on the sunny south wall'. The house is now used as offices of Christ Church University.

Betsey Trotwood's lawyer, Mr Wickfield, lived to the west of the city walls, beyond West Gate, at 71 St Dunstan's Street. It was a very old house bulging out over the road; a house with long low lattice-windows bulging out still further, and beams with carved heads on the ends bulging out too, so that I fancied the whole house was leaning forward, trying to see who was passing on the narrow pavement below. It was quite spotless in its cleanliness. The old-fashioned brass knocker on the low arched door, ornamented with carved garlands of fruit and flowers, twinkled like a star; the two stone steps descending to the door were as white as if they had been covered with fair linen; and all the angles and corners, and carvings and mouldings, and quaint little panes of glass, and quainter little windows, though as old as the hills, were as pure as any snow that ever fell upon the hills.

The house still fits Dickens's description and is called The House of Agnes, currently functioning as a hotel and restaurant. It is a seventeenth-century building but its history goes back to medieval times, having been a pilgrims' inn.

Not far away is North Lane, 100 yards or so around the corner, where Uriah Heep lived with his mother and where David Copperfield came on a visit. The alleged house has been demolished.

On another occasion Uriah was wandering on the eastern side of the city, on the Ramsgate road, when he overtook David, and made an appealing and eloquent explanation of his creepy, oleaginous character:

how little you think of the rightful umbleness of a person in my station, Master Copperfield! Father and me was both brought up at a foundation school for boys; and mother, she was likewise brought up at a public, sort of charitable, establishment. They taught us all a deal of umbleness – not much else that I know of, from morning to night. We was to be umble to this person, and umble to that, and to pull off our caps here, and to make bows there, and always to know our place, and abase ourselves before our betters. And we had such a lot of betters! ... 'Be umble, Uriah,' says father to me, 'and you'll get on.'

Wilkins Micawber, who, with uncharacteristic assiduity, worked to unmask Heep as a scheming villain, stayed at the Sun Hotel in Sun Street, described as a 'little inn'. The Micawbers economised and 'occupied a little room ... partitioned off from the commercial room, and strongly flavoured with tobacco smoke. I think it was over the kitchen, because a warm, greasy smell appeared to come up through the chinks in the floor, and there was a flabby perspiration on the walls. I know it was near the bar, on account of the smell of spirits and jingling of glasses'. The hotel survives and flourishes as a hotel and restaurant, though it does not quote the description of the Micawbers' room in its promotional literature. It has been completely refurbished in the last few years, and offers four-poster beds, but no parking facilities. Mr Micawber had dreams of his son becoming a chorister at Canterbury Cathedral, but his son's career took him no further than singing comic songs in public houses.

Dickens came to Canterbury in 1861 to give a reading. He stayed at the Fountain Inn. This used to be one of the great historic hotels of the city, claiming a history going back to the eleventh century, but it was destroyed by enemy action during the Second World War.

On Dickens's final visit in 1869 he brought friends to the city. They entered the cathedral, where a service was just starting. It seemed to be conducted in a casual manner. 'The seeming indifference of the officiating clergy', recalled one of the party, 'jarred most acutely on Dickens's feelings, for he, who did all things so thoroughly, could not conceive how (as he afterwards said) any persons accepting an office, or a trust so important as the proper rendering of our beautiful Cathedral Service, could go through their duties in this mechanical and slip-shod fashion.' Perhaps Dickens was in a testy mood, for a little later he became impatient with a 'tedious verger' who was showing the party around, shook him off and conducted his guests himself around the place 'in the most genial and learned style in the world.'

Staplehurst

No imagination can conceive the ruin of the carriages, or the extraordinary weights under which the people were lying, or the complications into which they were twisted up among iron and wood, and mud and water.

By THE MIDDLE of the 1860s, when he was not on tour giving his readings, Dickens was spending much of his time in France. He set up retreats for Nelly Ternan and himself, probably in Boulogne, Paris and Normandy – Dickens covered his tracks well and much is still conjecture.

On Friday morning, 9 June 1865, he travelled from France back to London. He boarded the ferry from Boulogne. An unsympathetic observer, the wife of an American press owner, spotted him 'travelling with not his wife, nor his sister-in-law, yet he strutted about the deck with the air of a man bristling with self-importance, every line of his face and every gesture of his limbs seemed haughtily to say, "Look at me; make the most of your chance. I am the great, the *only* Charles Dickens; whatever I may choose to do is justified by that fact".'

He was actually travelling with Nelly Ternan and her mother. They caught the boat train, operated by the South Eastern Railway Company, heading for London, which left

Folkestone at 14:38. It reached Headcorn at 15:11. The train times then varied according to the tide.

Dickens, Nelly and Mrs Ternan were in a first-class compartment, in the first of seven first-class coaches. They were immediately behind the engine and tender and one second-class coach. Behind the first-class coaches were two more second-class coaches and three luggage vans. The train was not crowded; there were 115 passengers altogether, 80 in first-class, 35 in second.

Between Headcorn and Staplehurst the line goes over the River Beult twice. There was – and is – a small viaduct over the river at the second crossing. In the early summer of 1865 some wooden baulks of the viaduct were being replaced. This required the temporary removal of the railway lines. The work was carried out in the periods when there was no train expected, the rails being put back in position for the passage of trains. The work was mostly completed, but on this Friday a gang was still at work. The gang foreman, Henry Benge, somehow thought it was Saturday, and was not expecting a train for another two hours. Nor did he have on him a watch. It was the job of a flagman to be 1000 yards from any obstruction, in the event of any train unexpectedly approaching. On this day he was only 500 yards from the work on the viaduct. The track here was a long and straight stretch, and as the train was not due not to stop until it reached Redhill, it was travelling at a full speed of between 40 and 50 miles an hour. The flagman saw the train and desperately flagged it down. The brakes were applied and the train was able to slow down to about 30 miles an hour. Five of the coaches also had brakes and these were applied. But a train travelling at 45 miles an

The Staplehurst Railway Accident

hour would travel the 500 yards between where the first signal was received and the viaduct in twenty seconds. At 30 miles an hour it would take thirty seconds. There was not enough time or distance for the train to come to a complete stop before the viaduct.

The momentum of the moving train carried the engine over the first part of the viaduct before it ground to a halt. The tender and the front two carriages, one second-class and the first-class one carrying Dickens and the Ternans, came to a stop at a giddy angle over the river. The next first-class carriage broke away and tumbled the ten feet onto the dry bed of the river, bottom up, bringing down the following carriages, which fell into mud and water, either on their sides or on top of each other. The last carriages, including the guard's van, remained coupled together on the Headcorn side of the viaduct.

Confusion and terror. Dickens and the Ternans were in a locked compartment. At the moment of the disaster, they were all thrown together as the compartment tilted alarmingly. 'Let us join hands and die together', Nelly is reported to have said. The train came to a halt. Dickens clambered out of the window and hailed two guards. With their help Dickens extricated the ladies from the compartment and got them away from the train. Nelly was slightly injured. In the panic to get out of the compartment she left her jewellery behind. The railway officials were able to look after Nelly and her mother. Meanwhile, Dickens climbed back into the compartment and brought out his brandy-flask and top hat. He was able to fill his top hat with water – where from? Was there a tap at the bridge? Or on the train? Or did he scoop up water from the stream? 'I was in the terrific Staplehurst accident yesterday', he wrote the next day to John Forster, 'and worked for hours among the dying and dead. I was in the carriage that did not go over, but went off the line, and hung over the bridge in an inexplicable manner. No words can describe the scene', he added.

Ten people were killed in the accident and many were seriously injured. Dickens and the Ternans were lucky to be relatively unscathed physically. For two hours Dickens moved among the dead and wounded providing succour. He helped to get one man out of 'a most extraordinary heap of dark ruins in which he was jammed upside down'. Having helped a number, he clambered back into his still-swaying compartment to retrieve the latest manuscript instalment of *Our Mutual Friend*. The instalment included the tale of Mr and Mrs Lammle, a couple, each of whom was penniless and married the other believing they were marrying money.

Railway officials and medical assistance were soon on the scene. Many people were reluctant to disclose their names, anxious not to spread alarm among friends and family. A relief train came and took passengers on to London.

Dickens returned to London and stayed for two nights at his bachelor flat in Wellington Street, before returning to the tranquillity of Gad's Hill Place. He was met at Higham Station by his son, Charley, who drove him up to Gad's Hill in the pony and trap. He was a nervous passenger, anxious even at the speed of the pony, 'Go slower, Charley', he constantly exhorted, until they were travelling at less than walking pace. He stayed at Gad's Hill Place for three months recovering, during which time he wrote to the station master at Charing Cross asking after the golden trinkets that Nelly had left behind in the compartment. One had *Ellen* engraved on it. Dickens had been badly shaken:

> I cannot bear railway travelling yet. A perfect conviction, against the senses, that the carriage is down on one side (and generally that is the left, and *not* the side on which the carriage in the accident really went over), comes upon me with anything like speed, and is inexpressibly distressing.

Dickens was most anxious to avoid the Ternans' names being disclosed. An official enquiry was held; Dickens declined to give evidence. An inquest on the ten dead passengers was held at the Railway Tavern, Staplehurst, and concluded that there was culpable negligence on the part of the gang leader, Henry

Benge, and also a supervisor, Joseph Gallimore, who had, in recent months, carried out insufficient checks. They were both committed for trial. Gallimore was acquitted and Benge sentenced to nine months' hard labour. The death certificates recorded the cause of death as 'feloniously killed by Joseph Gallimore and Henry Benge'.

The accident had a profound effect on Dickens for the rest of his life. Only his closest friends knew that he had been with Nelly. He had not only had a narrow escape from death, but also from scandal. He was able to travel by train, but not in express trains, which slowed down his travel as he resumed his reading tours. He was for evermore a nervous passenger. 'My reading secretary and companion knows so well when one of these odd momentary seizures comes upon me in a railway carriage, that he instantly produces a dram of brandy, which rallies the blood to the heart and generally prevails.'

The accident occurred on a Friday, always seen by Dickens as an auspicious day – it had been the day of his birth. But the date would come to take on even greater significance, as 9 June was the day of his death, five years later.

There is not much to be seen today that can remind us of the accident. The bridge over the river – hardly a viaduct, as some reports said – is away from the road or any public footpath. Trains rush over the bridge four times an hour during the daytime. The most economic and effective way of seeing the site is to take a day return ticket between Headcorn and Staplehurst. Some of the locals know about the accident, but not about the location of the inquest. Perhaps a plaque or two are due.

Bibliography

Dickens's works

I have used the Penguin Classics series. I have also used other editions of other works, such as *A Child's History of England*, *The Christmas Stories*, *Master Humphrey's Clock*, *Reprinted Pieces* and *The Uncommercial Traveller*. The Penguin Classics editions are as follows, in chronological order of composition, with the original date of publication in brackets after the title, followed by the name of the editor of that volume in the series.

Sketches by Boz (1839), Dennis Walder, 1995.
The Pickwick Papers (1836–37), Mark Wormald, 2000.
Oliver Twist (1837–38), Philip Horne, 2003.
Nicholas Nickleby (1839), Mark Ford, 1999.
The Old Curiosity Shop (1841), Norman Page, 2001.
Barnaby Rudge (1841), John Bowen, 2003.
A Christmas Carol and Other Christmas Writings (1835–54), Michael Slater, 2003.
Martin Chuzzlewit (1843–44), Patricia Ingham, 1999.
Dombey and Son (1848), Andrew Sanders, 2002.
David Copperfield (1850), Jeremy Tambling, 2004.
Bleak House (1853), Nicola Bradbury, 2003.
Hard Times (1854), Kate Flint, 2003.

Little Dorrit (1857), Stephen Wall, 1998 & Helen Small, 2003.
A Tale of Two Cities (1859), Richard Maxwell, 2007.
Great Expectations (1860–61), Charlotte Mitchell, 2003.
Our Mutual Friend (1865), Adrian Poole, 1997.
The Mystery of Edwin Drood (1870), David Paroissien, 2002.
Selected Journalism 1850–1870, David Pascoe, 2006.
Selected Short Fiction, Deborah A Thomas, 1976.

I have also consulted the Pilgrim Edition of the *Letters of Charles Dickens*, edited by Madeline House, Graham Storey and Kathleen Tillotson, 12 volumes, Oxford University Press, 1965–2002, and the Dickens Fellowship's Journal, *The Dickensian* (1905–).

Other works

Ackroyd, Peter, *Dickens* (London, 1990).
Ackroyd, Peter, *Thames, Sacred River* (London, 2007).
Ackroyd, Peter, *Wilkie Collins* (London, 2012).
Addison, William, *In the Steps of Charles Dickens* (London, 1955).
Adrian, Arthur A., *Georgina Hogarth and the Dickens Circle* (Oxford, 1957).
Allbut, Robert, *Rambles in Dickens-Land* (London, c. 1902).
Aylmer, Felix, *Dickens Incognito* (London, 1959).
Aylmer, Felix, *The Drood Case* (London, 1964).
Barlow, Eleanor Poe, *The Master's Cat: The Story of Charles Dickens as Told by his Cat* (London, 1998).
Burke, Thomas, *Travel in England* (London, 1942).

Carey, John, *The Violent Effigy: A Study of Dickens' Imagination* (London, 1973).

Cawthorne, Bob, *The Isle of Thanet Compendium* (Broadstairs, 2007).

Chesterton, G. K., *Charles Dickens* (London, 1928, first published 1906).

Clark, Peter (ed.), *The Lefties' Guide to Britain* (London, 2005).

Collins, Philip (ed.), *Dickens, Interviews and Recollections*, 2 vols. (London, 1981).

Daniell, Timothy, *Inns of Court* (London, 1985, first published 1971).

Davies, James A., *John Forster: A Literary Life* (Leicester, 1983).

Dexter, Walter, *The Kent of Dickens* (London, 1924).

Dickens, Henry, *The Recollections of Sir Henry Dickens, KG* (London, 1934).

Dickens, Mamie, *My Father as I Recall Him* (Westminster, 1897).

Dolby, George, *Charles Dickens as I Knew Him* (London, 1885).

Elsna, Hebe, *Unwanted Wife: A Defence of Mrs Charles Dickens* (London, 1963).

Fitzgerald, Percy, *Bozland: Dickens' Places and People* (London, 1895).

Forster, John, *The Life of Charles Dickens*, 2 vols. (London and Toronto, 1927, first published 1872–4).

Gadd, W. Laurence, *The Great Expectations Country* (London, 1929).

Handbook for Travellers in Kent, 5th edition (London, 1892).

Hardwick, Michael and Mollie, *The Charles Dickens Encyclopedia* (London, 1976).

Hardwick, Michael and Mollie, *Dickens's England* (London, 1970).

Heffernan, Hilary, *Hop Pickers of Kent and Sussex* (Stroud, 2008).

Hibbert, Christopher, *The Making of Charles Dickens* (London, 1968, first published 1967).

House, Humphry, *The Dickens World* (Oxford, 1941).

Hughes, William R., *A Week's Tramp in Dickens-Land* (London, 1891).

Jackson, T. A., *Charles Dickens: The Progress of a Radical* (London, 1937).

Jessup, Frank W., *Kent History Illustrated* (Maidstone, 1966).

Johnson, Edgar, *Charles Dickens: His Tragedy and Triumph*, 2 vols. (London, 1953).

Kitton, Frederic G., *Charles Dickens: His Life, Writings and Personality* (London, nd).

Kitton, Frederic G., *The Dickens' Country* (London, 1911, first published 1905).

Lane, Anthony, *Thames-side Kent Through Time* (Stroud, 2011).

Langton, Robert, *The Childhood and Youth of Charles Dickens* (Manchester, 1883).

Lazarus, Mary, *A Tale of Two Brothers: Charles Dickens's Sons in Australia* (Sydney, 1973).

Macaskill, Hilary, *Charles Dickens at Home* (London, 2011).

MacDougall, Philip, *Chatham Through Time* (Stroud, 2011).

Margate Delineated, 10th edition (Margate, 1829).

Matz, B. W., *Dickensian Inns and Taverns* (London, 1922, first published 1921).

Matz, B. W., *The Inns and Taverns of 'Pickwick'* (London, nd).

Nayder, Lillian, *The Other Dickens: A Life of Catherine Hogarth* (Ithaca, NY, 2012).

Newman, John, *The Buildings of England: North East and East Kent* (Harmondsworth, 1976, first published 1969).

Newman, John, *The Buildings of England: West Kent and the Weald* (Harmondsworth, 1969).

Nicklin, J. A. and Haslehust, E. W., *Dickens-Land* (London and Glasgow, nd).

Nisbet, Ada, *Dickens and Ellen Ternan* (Berkeley and Los Angeles, 1952).

Rimmer, Alfred, *About England with Dickens* (London, 1883).

Slater, Michael, *Charles Dickens* (New Haven and London, 2009).

Slater, Michael, *The Great Charles Dickens Scandal* (New Haven and London, 2012).

Smith, Lynda, *The Place to Spend a Happy Day: A History of Rosherville Gardens* (Gravesend, 2006).

Solnit, Rebecca, *Wanderlust, A History of Walking* (New York, 2000).

Storey, Gladys, *Dickens and Daughter* (London, 1939).

Tomalin, Claire, *Charles Dickens, A Life* (London, 2011).

Tomalin, Claire, *The Invisible Woman, The Story of Nelly Ternan and Charles Dickens* (London, 1991).

Ward, A. W., Dickens (London, 1882).

Watts, Alan S., *Dickens at Gad's Hill* (Goring-on-Thames, 1989).

Wright, Christopher, *Kent Through the Years* (London, 1975).

Acknowledgements

Eddie Ault; Lee Ault; Patricia Barbor; Peter Barbor; Andrew Bryant; Christoph Bull; Pamela Bunney; Kevin Christie; Pearl Cooper; Jeremy Goad; Phillida Goad; Ayaan Mahamdallie; Hassan Mahamdallie; Nicola Hilton; John Knott; Sean Magee; Jane Martin; Robin Martin; Steve Martin; Judith Newberry; John Peverley; Ian Porter; John Rushworth; Zoë Rutherford; Eve Smith; Les Stather; Charlotte Taylor; Andrew Thompson; Ionis Thompson; Kat Whone; and Fernando at the George and Vulture Inn, London.

Above all I wish to thank Theresa, who gave constructive comment on the text and accompanied me on several tours of Dickens sites in London and Kent.

Acknowledgements